Strategic Board Recruitment

The Not-for-Profit Model

Robert W. Kile

J. Michael Loscavio

Editor: Jamie Whaley

An ASPEN PUBLICATION®

ISBN# 0-8342-0797-4

❏ INTRODUCTION

Board recruitment is one of the most important and least understood functions of nonprofit boards. The search for new board members often involves well-intentioned volunteers, with little or no recruiting experience, contacting well-intentioned candidates with little or no board experience.

It is understandable that nominating committee members find it easier and less intimidating to contact individuals personally known or recommended by other board members. Yet, their approach to finding suitable candidates is reminiscent of Inspector Renault's in the movie, *Casablanca*. When asked how he intended to solve the most recent case, the Inspector replied, "Round up the usual suspects."

The usual suspects, or circle-of-friends, approach to board recruitment is too limited in today's competitive nonprofit environment, where leadership, fund development, diversity and vision are essential to succeed.

To be effective, recruiting must be a continuous process rather than a series of isolated events. *Strategic Board Recruitment: The Not-for-Profit Model* is based on the process, systems and techniques used by executive search professionals. It is written to help nonprofit volunteer teams strengthen their boards, by providing them with a framework for executing and institutionalizing a results-oriented recruitment process.

A systematic approach to board member recruitment gets results

To build the best possible organization, board members need the expertise and connections that will help it reach its goals. For example, if your organization's goal is to raise $10 million over three years, the board will be best served by members with fund raising experience and connections to major donors in the community. A board without these types of members may reach the goal, but its path to success is likely to be marked by time- and resource-consuming trial and error.

In most cases, the right people for your board won't just come to you and ask, "May I join?" You have to go into the community and find them. And this is why you need to systematically identify, approach and recruit well-qualified, high-profile, high-energy people to serve on your board.

Aspen Publishers' *Strategic Board Recruitment: The Not-for-Profit Model* can help you improve your current recruiting techniques. As the title implies, it will also show you how to add board members strategically and create the ideal mix of talent and skills your board needs to reach its full potential.

The model also is unique because it sets up a process that will become part and parcel of how your nonprofit operates. The components of the system are organized to outlive your current board—so when the next generation of board members takes over, the recruiting structure, contacts and process are already in place. New members can pick up where past members left off, rather than starting over with their own personal contacts.

Overview of the eight-step process

The strategic recruitment process described in this manual is a cumulative eight-step process. Each step builds on the previous one.

Here's a brief summary of each:

Step 1) Assembling the board development team. To recruit strategically, your organization should replace the board's traditional nominating committee with a board development team. This team is made up of the executive director, board chairperson, fund development professional and up to three other high-profile board or staff members or volunteers.

The development team is responsible for making the recruitment process work. For example, team members align the

organization's plans and goals, develop the overall recruitment strategy, write a recruiting action plan, conduct research on prospective board members and guide prospects through the recruiting process. The team is also responsible for regularly reporting its progress to the full board. The full board selects the best candidates to serve on the board.

Step 2) Assessing the organization's needs. To find the best board candidates, the development team must determine which skills and clout the board needs to reach the organization's goals.

This is accomplished in two phases: an alignment of goals stated in the strategic, operational and fund development plans; and an inventory of current board members' skills and resources. The results of these assessments are used to develop a strategy for recruiting prospects who meet specific organization needs.

Step 3) Developing board position profiles. Before contacting prospects for any board vacancy, the development team must decide what qualifications and skills it's looking for. For example, how many years of experience will the ideal "marketing" board member have in the field? Must he or she have a nonprofit background? What types of projects would you prefer this person have experience in planning and conducting?

After the qualifications for each board slot are determined, they should be organized in a position profile. This document describes the scope of the position, the ideal experience and skills, key duties and responsibilities, expectations and key priorities of the job. The development team uses the profiles to identify qualified board candidates.

Step 4) Scripting the organization's

story. The board development team is also responsible for preparing a script that members can refer to when contacting prospects.

Scripts include a review of the nonprofit's history and mission, its programs, future plans and the expected outcome of implementing those plans. They can also be used to develop a marketing piece or brochure that can be used for recruiting and other community relations activities.

Step 5) Researching candidate sources. With position profiles and scripted story in hand, the board development team develops a list of candidates. Traditionally, these have been friends of board members.

The development team should expand its research to include other candidate sources—like members and patrons of the organization and donors. Team members should also take advantage of researched sources, such as professional associations, as places to find qualified board candidates.

Step 6) Developing third-party referral networks. Every organization could benefit from establishing relationships in the community that provide board candidate referrals and information that helps the nonprofit achieve its goals. These relationships are called third-party referral networks.

To establish a network, potential members—like banks, corporations or universities—are best identified early in the recruiting process. The network relationship can then be pursued two ways...

The development team can begin establishing a relationship with networks by discussing the board position with their members, employees or representatives and asking for any possible referrals. This initial telephone relationship will be gradually nurtured into a standing affiliation between the target firms and your nonprofit.

Sometimes, the development team may recruit board prospects directly from these organizations. After individuals from these circles are securely on board, the team continues nurturing its relationship with these new members, and eventually builds a second and permanent relationship between the nonprofit and these board members' organizations.

Step 7) Contacting and meeting candidates. When contacting potential board candidates, development team members will use all the tools developed earlier in the recruitment process.

For example, during team members' first contacts with prospects, they'll describe the ideal board candidate using the position profile. Later, during personal meetings with interested board prospects, team members will ask interview questions based on the profile.

Step 8) Evaluating and selecting new board members. A final recommendation decision is never based solely on the initial interview. If candidates are interested in learning more about a board position, they're invited to attend nonprofit activities and participate on short-term committees.

This gives the board development team additional time to evaluate candidates, and it gives candidates more time to decide if they want to be part of the nonprofit's future.

Editor's Note: A visual summary of the process is on Page ix.

Process may mean new board practices

This strategic recruitment model is more than just a system to help you bring the most-qualified people onto your organization's board. It also presents a new way of using nonprofit board members to help the organization reach its goals.

This change is most evident in the board committee system. To take full advantage of the strategic recruitment system, you may have to change some traditional committee practices.

For example, most board committees are standing committees that exist year-round. Members of these committees, who are also board members, serve for a designated term, usually a year, then rotate off.

To recruit strategically, this committee structure should be adjusted in two ways:

First, committee membership should be extended to non-board members.

An essential part of the recruitment process involves placing qualified board member candidates on board committees or teams. Committee service gives candidates a chance to get to know the organization and how it works. It also gives the board development team an opportunity to watch the candidate complete projects and interact with current board members. Then based on candidates' performance with committee projects, the development team chooses nominees for the full board. This process makes such a change in committee structure both necessary and practical.

Second, some committees or teams should be formed only to complete specific goal-related projects—like organizing a fund raiser or writing a new marketing plan. This change increases the full board's flexibility.

Since its members aren't consumed by their obligations to various standing committees, the board can quickly set up a team to tackle a new challenge. Plus, the temporary nature of these teams allows the organization to benefit from the skills of individuals who do want to make a contribution to the nonprofit, but who don't want to make a long-term commitment to board service.

Together, these changes give recruiting a new and different "look." The goal of the process remains the same—to always have members with quality skills and connections on the board. The process of choosing them, however, is different.

Instead of immediately asking a prospect to serve on the board—as many nominating committees do—the strategic recruiting model promotes building relationships with well-qualified individuals by involving them in board activities. Then, at the appropriate time, these candidates will be invited to become full board members.

Strategic Board Recruitment Model offers long-term benefits

Changing your recruiting habits from the traditional nominating committee approach to the strategic approach will take a lot of organization and commitment. However, the benefits of strategic recruiting are well worth the effort. For example...

■ **You'll get the people you want for the board.** Some boards accept candidates because they're convenient—not necessarily because they're the best people for the job. For example, a board might accept a candidate with limited marketing skills as chairperson of that committee because he or she is the only person current board members know in that profession.

Using the strategic recruiting process, however, you won't be faced with this situation. You'll be able to identify and recruit a number of experienced marketing professionals who can deliver the marketing "products" and results your nonprofit needs.

This is sometimes called the rifle approach to recruiting, as opposed to the shotgun approach. Instead of asking many prospects to join the board and hoping that one of them will accept (like a shotgun, which fires a spray of pellets), you can zero in on specific candidates and then court them through the process (like a rifle, which fires a single bullet).

■ **You'll be able to recruit higher-profile people to the board.** To elevate the overall level of your board, you have to elevate the level of the members serving on the recruiting team. That means placing the top people in your organization on this team.

High-profile individuals are impressed by organizations that have clear goals and well-organized plans for achieving them. When you approach them with the strategic recruiting process and specific ideas about how you can use their skills, they are more likely to help you.

■ **You'll get cooperation from people who can't sit on the board.** Even if highly qualified candidates can't find enough time to join your nonprofit's board, the flexible committee or team structure still allows them to contribute.

For example, very busy, high-profile individuals who can't commit to a full two- or three-year board term—or who aren't interested in being a full board member—may be willing to help you for shorter periods of time. By offering them positions on specific project committees, you can reap the benefits of these individuals' skills and experience.

■ **You'll get better results from the board.** If you have people with the skills to help your board and its committees accomplish goals, those individuals will motivate the board or committee to reach them.

The high-profile candidates you're seeking are efficient, productive workers. Assignments given to them will be completed on or ahead of schedule—which means your board will be able to solve problems quickly and progress decisively toward its goals.

Bylaw changes reflect new philosophy

For many boards, the process of recruitment and installation is spelled out by bylaws.

Adopting the strategic recruiting process may mean adopting a new set of bylaws—a set that describes the new players and procedures. For example, summaries of nominating committee responsibilities should be changed to reflect the role of the board development team. Bylaws may also have to be modified to allow non-board members to serve as members of board committees.

Changing bylaws represents a major change in philosophy and procedure. It sends a message to the entire organization that the board is fully committed to a new approach.

Moving forward without first making these bylaw changes can set the board up to fail. Without a formal, open commitment to the strategic recruiting process, it becomes easy for the development team to slip backwards—and resume doing things the old way. A formal change in bylaws motivates development team members to make the new strategic recruiting process work.

Definition of terms

Because the strategic recruitment process differs from the traditional nominating committee method, it makes sense to clarify the meaning of some terms. Here are three common terms and how they will be used throughout this manual:

■ **Board member source.** This is the individual, a group or other organization that gives you the name of a potential board candidate. The source, however, is not the person being evaluated as a possible board member.

■ **Board member candidate.** This is a prospect who is well into the evaluation process. A candidate is a person who is seriously interested in the board position and will be considered for recommendation.

■ **Volunteer.** When the term "volunteer" is used in this manual, it will apply to the high-profile board prospects who help the board in some way.

For example, Chapter 8 reviews how board member candidates are often placed on board committees. These candidates are considered volunteers. They're donating their time and skills to the organization on either a short-term basis, or serving as ongoing members of one specific committee.

A special thank you

A special note of thanks is extended to the executive team, professional staff and board members at the Mid-America Chapter of the American Red Cross in Chicago, Illinois.

They have done a significant amount of work with this strategic recruiting model and helped in refining many of the concepts it employs. Because of this, the model continues to grow in use and effectiveness, and the detail of this book is possible. ■

VISUAL SUMMARY: THE EIGHT-STEP RECRUITMENT PROCESS

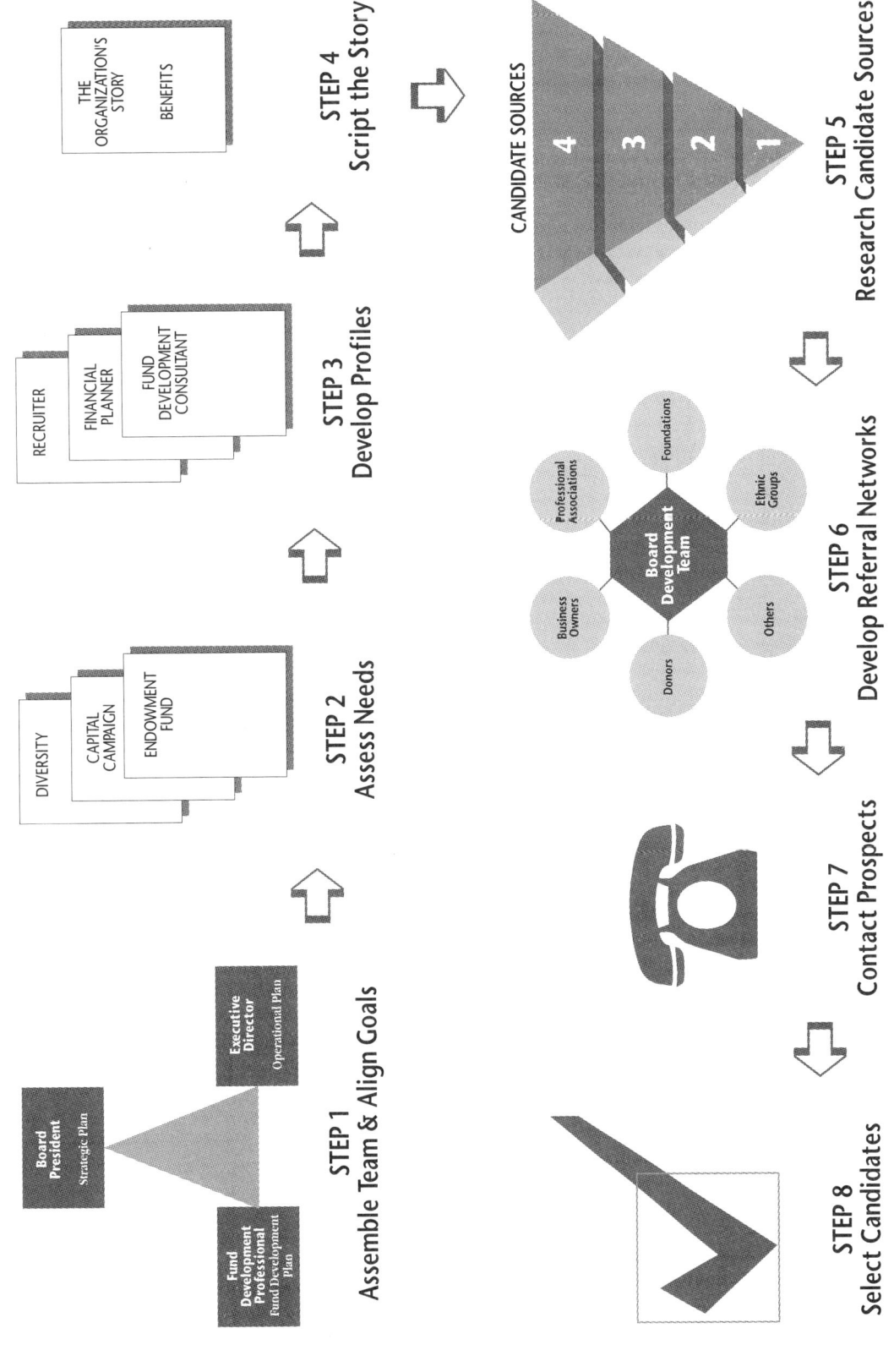

Board President
Strategic Plan

Executive Director
Operational Plan

Fund Development Professional
Fund Development Plan

STEP 1
Assemble Team & Align Goals

DIVERSITY
CAPITAL CAMPAIGN
ENDOWMENT FUND

STEP 2
Assess Needs

RECRUITER
FINANCIAL PLANNER
FUND DEVELOPMENT CONSULTANT

STEP 3
Develop Profiles

THE ORGANIZATION'S STORY
BENEFITS

STEP 4
Script the Story

CANDIDATE SOURCES
4
3
2
1

STEP 5
Research Candidate Sources

Board Development Team
Professional Associations
Foundations
Ethnic Groups
Others
Donors
Business Owners

STEP 6
Develop Referral Networks

STEP 7
Contact Prospects

STEP 8
Select Candidates

Table of Contents

INTRODUCTION

TABLE OF CONTENTS

CHAPTER 1: Assemble the Board Development Team

Why a development team? **5**
Problems with nominating committees 5
Name change improves results 6
Convince board a change is necessary 6
Change board bylaws when called for 7
Development team structure **7**
The development team's "hub" should remain constant 8
Development team needs a captain... 8
Goal of development team... 9
How the development team relates to the full board 10
STOP! Procedure checkpoint 11
      Board Development Team Hub 12
      The Board Development Team 13

CHAPTER 2: Assess the Organization's Needs

Conduct a needs assessment **19**
Step #1: Align the organization's goals **19**
Why bring goals together?... 19
Alignment is like a boat... 20
How goal alignment is accomplished 20
Modify goals if necessary 21
Step #2: Inventory board members' skills **21**
Matrix measures board members' skills 22
Using the assessment matrix 22

The board assessment process 23
Interpreting assessment results 23
Measuring staff needs 23
Step #3: Develop a recruiting strategy **24**
Recruiting strategy thought process 24
Recruiting strategy provides short- and long-term benefits 25
Step #4: Prepare a formal action plan **26**
Warning: Take your time developing the action plan 27
Report finalized action plan to the whole organization... 27
Ongoing assessments keep recruiting strategy up-to-date 28
STOP! Procedure checkpoint 29
    Board Profile/Assessment Matrix (Table 1) 30
    Board Profile/Assessment Matrix (Table 2) 31
    Board Profile/Assessment Matrix (Table 3) 32
    Current Board Member Names 33
    Action Plan Template 34

CHAPTER 3: Develop Board Position Profiles

Position profile structure **41**
Assessment results and goals provide a starting point 41
Key positions help build your board 41
Content of position profiles 42
Element #1: Scope 42
Element #2: Experience and skills 42
Element #3: Key duties and responsibilities 42
Element #4: Expectations 43
Element #5: Key priorities 43
Profile development process **44**
Begin profile development with brainstorming sessions 44
Computer simplifies writing process 45
Position profiles yield future benefits 45
Profiles guide board referrals 46
STOP! Procedure checkpoint 47
    Position Profile Template 48
    Sample Position Profile 50

CHAPTER 4: Script the Organization's Story

Scripts provide information **57**
Elements of effective scripts 57
Element #1: Charter, mission, purpose 57

Element #2: Nonprofit services 57
Element #3: Current and future plans 58
Element #4: Expected outcomes 58
Element #5: The eight-step professional recruitment process 58
Write effective scripts **59**
Features and benefits encourage prospect involvement 60
Create an emotional hook 60
CASE STUDY: Emotional hook gets prospects involved 61
Tell prospects who's on the board too 61
Script format retains presentation flexibility 62
Script-writing procedure resembles profile-writing process 62
Benefits of script use **63**
CASE STUDY: Scripts give team members direction 64
STOP! Procedure checkpoint 65
    Scripted Story Template 66
    Features and Benefits Template 68
    Sample Marketing Piece/Brochure 69

CHAPTER 5: Research Board Candidate Sources

Recruit from multiple sources **79**
Why recruit from all levels? 79
Level #1: Friends and colleagues 80
Level #2: Members and patrons of your nonprofit 80
Level #3: Donors and contributors 80
Level #4: Researched sources 81
Accessing researched sources **81**
Where to start when you don't know what to do first 82
Phone tips for contacting potential candidate sources 83
Third-party referrals make candidate research easier 83
Leverage contacts for best referrals 84
How many contacts are needed? 84
Fund development professional researches candidates... 84
Secure the fund development professional's help 85
When there's no fund development professional to call upon 85
Past prospects provide additional candidate sources 86
Keep records of contacts **86**
Computers simplify record keeping 87
STOP! Procedure checkpoint 87
    Potential Board Candidate Sources 89
    Targeted Board Recruitment Call Lists 90

CHAPTER 6: Develop Third-Party Referral Networks

Referral networks defined **95**
How nonprofits use referral networks 95
Developing a referral network 96
Target the best companies and organizations for a network 96
Institutionalize network relationships **97**
Create relationships slowly 97
Build a referral network without adding board members 98
Beneficial affiliations for all networks 98
Referral networks outlive traditional nominating committee networks 98
Second-generation development teams expand network 99
STOP! Procedure checkpoint 100
    Structure of a Network 101
    Evolution of a Network 102

CHAPTER 7: Contact and Meet Candidate Prospects

Start the contact process **107**
Group meetings are most productive 107
How to meet highest-profile prospects 107
The first contact: An introductory telephone call 108
Tips for successful telephone contacts 108
Sample telephone conversation 110
Redirect the phone call when contacts seem uninterested 110
Move on after a negative contact 111
Use other recruitment tools to follow up telephone contacts 111
Practice makes interviews perfect 112
Conduct face-to-face meetings **112**
Let prospects share their feelings about the opportunity 113
When personal interviews go badly 114
Maintain records of all contacts **115**
Record information on Candidate Information Form 115
Development team reports 115
Continuous contacts give development team a choice 116
STOP! Procedure checkpoint 117
    Board Recruiting Contacts 118
    Board Candidate Information 119

CHAPTER 8: Evaluate and Select New Board Members

The evaluation process **125**

How to create contact and exposure 125
Questions reveal candidate qualities 126
Structured interviews provide results...126
Ask candidates to provide résumés 127
Present board member candidates with involvement options 127
Committees, short-term tasks get candidates involved 128
CASE STUDY: Value of strategic recruiting and flexibility 129
Long-term benefits of short-term project teams 129
When candidates want to immediately join the full board...130
Select and recommend new members 131
Candidate selection criteria 131
Recommend candidates to the board 131
First-time presentation expectations 132
Recommendations should be oral...132
Board member installation basics 133
Evaluating the recruitment process 133
STOP! Procedure checkpoint 134
  Interview Question Exercise 135
  Recruitment Process Evaluation Form...137

IN SUMMARY

ABOUT THE AUTHORS

CHAPTER

Assemble the Board Development Team

Why a development team? **5**
Problems with nominating committees 5
Name change improves results 6
Convince board a change is necessary 6
Change board bylaws when called for 7
Development team structure **7**
The development team's "hub" should remain constant 8
Development team needs a captain... 8
Goal of development team.. 9
How the development team relates to the full board 10
STOP! Procedure checkpoint 11
    Board Development Team Hub 12
    The Board Development Team 13

CHAPTER

Assemble the Board Development Team

To set the wheels of strategic recruitment in motion, your nonprofit's board will probably need to make some changes in its traditional recruitment practices. It should begin, for example, by reassigning all recruiting responsibilities to a specially designed board development team. ■ This team leads the recruiting process and is made up of both board members and non-board members. Its responsibilities include identifying the organization's needs, finding individuals who can fill them and, over time, developing and maintaining a board that will move the nonprofit toward its goals. Hence the word "development" in the team's title. ■ This chapter explains more about these tasks and the board development team itself—including who should be on it and why it's an essential element of the strategic recruiting process. ■

❏ WHY A DEVELOPMENT TEAM?

Some nominating committees are effective. Many nominating committees, however, are not. They tend to do little recruiting work for much of the year, and then rush to find candidate names a month or two before new board members are scheduled for installation.

Often, these last-minute candidates are friends and acquaintances of current board members. Some have skills the board needs, while some don't. Few, if any, are formally interviewed and evaluated on well-defined criteria before being nominated. These candidates are often simply recommended, approved and installed. Committee members give little thought to how, or if, they will complement current board members, or to what impact these candidates may have on current board projects.

Problems with nominating committees

As a result of this haphazard nominating method, some nonprofit boards struggle to attain their goals. In fact, boards that recruit this way often encounter these problems:

■ **Board member performance doesn't measure up to expectations.** Some board members don't pull their weight when it comes to following through with their board responsibilities. They skip meetings, fail to do assignments and don't live up to commitments. These individuals are on the board in name, but not action.

This situation usually arises when board recruits aren't told specifically what is expected of them as members. Nominating

committees sometimes overlook this information in the race to find prospective candidates. They don't explain the depth of a commitment to the board—or give prospects opportunities to experience firsthand how the board works.

Instead, nominating committees talk about their organization's mission and what an honor and privilege it is to be part of it. Only after joining the board do new members realize that its demands—attending monthly meetings, serving on committees, raising money and contributing personally—are too much to handle. Gradually, the performance of these members slips to the sub-par level.

As a result of this partial participation, the board never reaches its full potential. To do that, the entire board membership must live up to its commitment and give a 100% effort.

■ **Board member skills and contacts tend to be limited.** Because nominating committees often need to locate board candidates quickly—and because these committees usually don't have a plan for finding quality prospects—members tend to approach only their circle of friends and acquaintances about serving on the board.

The problem with this is that although these friends and acquaintances may be seasoned professionals, they do not necessarily have the skills the board needs.

For example, a board member may have a friend who owns a business and who is a top-notch manager. The friend, however, knows nothing about fund raising. This person may be a valuable addition to the board, but he or she won't have the know-how and clout to solicit major gifts in a capital campaign.

■ **Second- and third-generation board members aren't as committed as their predecessors.** Founding board members have a genuine zeal for their nonprofit's mission. If they didn't, they never would have started the organization in the first place.

This high level of interest is difficult to maintain when second-, third- and fourth-generation board members come from the nominating committee members' friends. Often, these recruits join the board because of relationships with current board members. They want to be part of the same thing their friends are. They aren't, however, necessarily committed to making a difference in the lives of those the nonprofit serves.

When board members' hearts aren't in board service, boards lose momentum and consistency. As members rotate off the board, the friends they recruited may lose interest as well. These friends may stop attending or participating in meetings—and soon leave the board themselves.

Name change improves results

You may be wondering how changing a title from "nominating committee" to "board development team" can solve these problems.

To be honest, it can't. A name change alone won't guarantee fewer problems. It will, however, create a more positive attitude toward recruiting. And board members who are excited about recruiting get better results.

This change is directly related to the difference in connotation between the words "nominating" and "development."

The term "nominating committee," for instance, puts specific limits on its members.

To nominate means "to recommend for appointment." In the strictest sense, nominating is nothing more than putting a name on a table for confirmation.

This meaning is reflected in the nominating committee's work and attitude. The committee identifies and recommends individuals for board service. Committee members don't expect to do more than this—and they don't.

The title "board development team," however, implies a much broader responsibility. As before, this is reflected in the development team's actions. It creates and maintains a board capable of reaching specific goals—by determining what type of prospects to look for, collecting quality referrals, contacting prospects, building a relationship with them and, ultimately, recommending that the board accept them as new members. The name also implies that training and development activities will be available to board members after they've been selected.

The effect is that board development team members are more committed to their responsibilities. They know going into the recruitment process that their title demands more than just producing the names of three or four candidates. As a result, they follow through.

Convince board a change is necessary

Even though strategic recruitment will improve your board, it's not without risk. Adopting it, after all, sometimes means changing the way things have always been done.

Because of this, board members may hesitate to commit to the new system. They're already comfortable with the nominating committee, and they know that it works at least well enough to maintain the status quo.

To persuade hesitant board members that establishing a board development team is the right thing to do, focus your appeal on members' desire to improve the board's effectiveness. For example, explain how having an organized, strategic plan for finding, evaluating and selecting board candidates will generate a greater number of qualified candidates than the current nominating system. Over time, the strategic recruiting model can make the board more proactive and goal-oriented—which means it will be more effective.

Change board bylaws when called for

Most boards will be able to convert from a nominating committee to a board develop-ment team without making large-scale adjust-ments. Some boards, however, may have to alter their bylaws to facilitate the change in recruiting procedure.

For example, if a board's current bylaws don't allow staff members to serve on the nominating committee or board development team, they will need to be rewritten to include the executive director and fund development professional as members of the recruiting team. At large organizations this team often will include other key professional staff members, such as the director of volunteers, director of volunteer development and director of marketing.

A change in bylaws may also be necessary to formally change the nominating committee's name to board development team.

❏ DEVELOPMENT TEAM STRUCTURE

Obviously, the first step in creating an effective board development team is deciding who will be on it.

The typical development team should have no more than six members. Three of those positions are always filled by the same people: the organization's executive director, the board chairperson and, if the nonprofit has one, the fund development professional. If your organization doesn't have a full- or part-time development director, then include the board or staff's most effective fund raiser on the team. (Look at present and past chairpersons and members of the fund development committee for potential candidates.)

The remaining slots should be filled with people who have the ability to reach high-energy, high-profile board candidates. These team members could be high-ranking staff members, board members or volunteers. Past board presidents are excellent choices because they've been in a leadership role and have an established association with the nonprofit.

Specifically, look for individuals who have all-around abilities and a reputation for making things happen. Development team members must be oriented to results, have high profiles in the business community and have extensive personal contacts and clout. Without energetic and committed development team members, the chances are that the team as a whole won't live up to its potential.

Members' energy and status are important because it's difficult to improve the quality of your board without improving the quality of members serving on it.

People tend to be attracted to people who are like them. Therefore, a high-profile development team will appeal to high-profile candidates. On the other hand, a low-profile development team will appeal to less-qualified candidates. To get the best people, you must approach them with your best.

Prospective development team members should be approached in the same way you approach board member prospects: Explain what you're doing and then ask for their help in moving the nonprofit from Point A to Point B.

The development team's "hub" should remain constant

The executive director, board chairperson and fund development professional are the constant center of the development team and should always be part of team activities.

The team needs their input because they lead the three key arms of the nonprofit. The executive director oversees programs and staff, the board chairperson manages the board, and the fund development professional coordinates efforts to raise money.

As the nonprofit's leaders, the executive director, board chairperson and fund development professional are privy to the details of their respective responsibilities in the nonprofit's long-range plan. They know their goals and what must be accomplished to reach them.

Understanding these goals is vital to the board development team because it bases its decision about whom to recruit on what the organization needs. This is why it's so important that the executive director, board chairperson and fund development director always be part of the team. No one is more knowledgeable of their respective goals, or is in a better position to decide who can be of help in accomplishing them.

Development team needs a captain

Like all teams, the board development team will need a leader—someone to claim ownership of the process and keep group members focused on the tasks at hand.

Anyone on the team can assume this role. The person likely to be most effective, however, is the executive director.

As executive director, you have the largest stake in making the strategic recruitment process work. For instance, before presenting the eight-step recruitment process to board members, you've invested a good deal of time researching it. Persuading board members to adopt the model also requires time and effort. And because the board may have needed to make major changes to put the process in place, like amending its bylaws, you need to make it show dividends.

Improving the quality of new board members will also make your job as executive director easier. This is because board actions also affect the nonprofit programs you supervise. To improve and expand these services, executive directors need board members who can raise money, build the nonprofit's image and make significant strides toward long-range goals.

As a member of the development team, you can help guide the selection of new board members with the skills and connections to do these things. As a result, you'll spend less time working with board members to complete their projects—and you'll be able to concentrate on building the organization's programs for the future.

Goal of development team

The long-term goal of any board development team is to make sure the board is always made up of members who have the skills, connections and commitment to help your organization improve and grow.

To reach this goal, team members must focus their energy on four sub-goals, or objectives:

Objective #1) Identifying, recruiting and selecting board members and volunteers. This is the development team's primary job and the reason the team was formed.

The full board plays a relatively minor role in recruiting and selecting board members. The development team—with approval from the full board—starts the process by assessing the organization's goals and board member skills. From there, the team develops a profile of the candidate it's seeking, prepares a presentation for candidates, researches possible sources and then contacts them.

Regular board members will hear reports of the team's progress and recommend possible candidates. Their contact with prospects is minimal, however, until the development team involves board candidates in committee work.

Objective #2) Coordinating the organization's goals. Part of identifying appropriate board prospects is determining what skills those prospects must have. To do this, the board development team should regularly review the organization's goals as stated in the strategic, operational and fund development plans. It should also make sure that the executive director, board chairperson and fund development professional understand how the plans complement one another, and what each professional's arm of the nonprofit must accomplish in order for the others to reach their goals.

These activities show team members what the board, as a whole, needs to accomplish. They also tell the development team what skills to look for in board prospects. (Specific information about aligning the organization's goals is the subject of Chapter 2.)

Objective #3) Nurturing relationships between the community and the organization. In addition to recruiting quality board members, it's important that the development team build relationships with community groups, businesses and government organizations that can help the nonprofit.

These groups, called third-party referral networks, can provide the development team with quality board candidate referrals and information that can benefit the organization. (More about third-party referral networks is in Chapter 6.)

Objective #4) Orienting new board

members. Although it's not discussed in this manual, the development team may also assist in the new board member's orientation process. This is a logical step since the development team initiated the nonprofit's relationship with the individual.

How the development team relates to the full board

Although the board development team includes non-board members—the executive director and fund development professional—and isn't referred to as a "committee," it will relate to the full board much like a regular board committee. For example...

■ **It must report its activities to the full board.** Each month, the board development team prepares a report for the full board that briefs members on its activities and progress.

These reports typically include updates on how many new prospects have been contacted, how candidates are progressing through the evaluation process, board assessment results, profiles for open positions and summaries of other development team work.

■ **It lacks authority to make long-term decisions.** Although the board development team courts prospects through the selection process, it can only recommend them for a full board term. The team can't approve nominees on its own. All recommendations must be approved by the full board.

■ **It works independently to save the full board time and energy.** The board development team shoulders the entire responsibility for recruiting. Full board members may refer candidates to the team, but team members develop position profiles for openings, gather names, contact candidates and then evaluate them. The full board gets involved when the team's final choices are presented for approval. ■

STOP! Procedure checkpoint

Before moving on to Step 2 of the strategic recruiting process, Assess the Organization's Needs, have you...

❑ Presented the board development team concept to your board?

❑ Voted to adopt the development team system?

❑ Modified board bylaws as needed to form a development team?

❑ Established the hub of the board development team (executive director, board chairperson and fund development professional)?

❑ Carefully chosen the remaining members of the development team?

❑ Selected an individual to captain the development team?

❑ Reviewed the development team's goals with all team members?

BOARD DEVELOPMENT TEAM HUB

Core Team Members

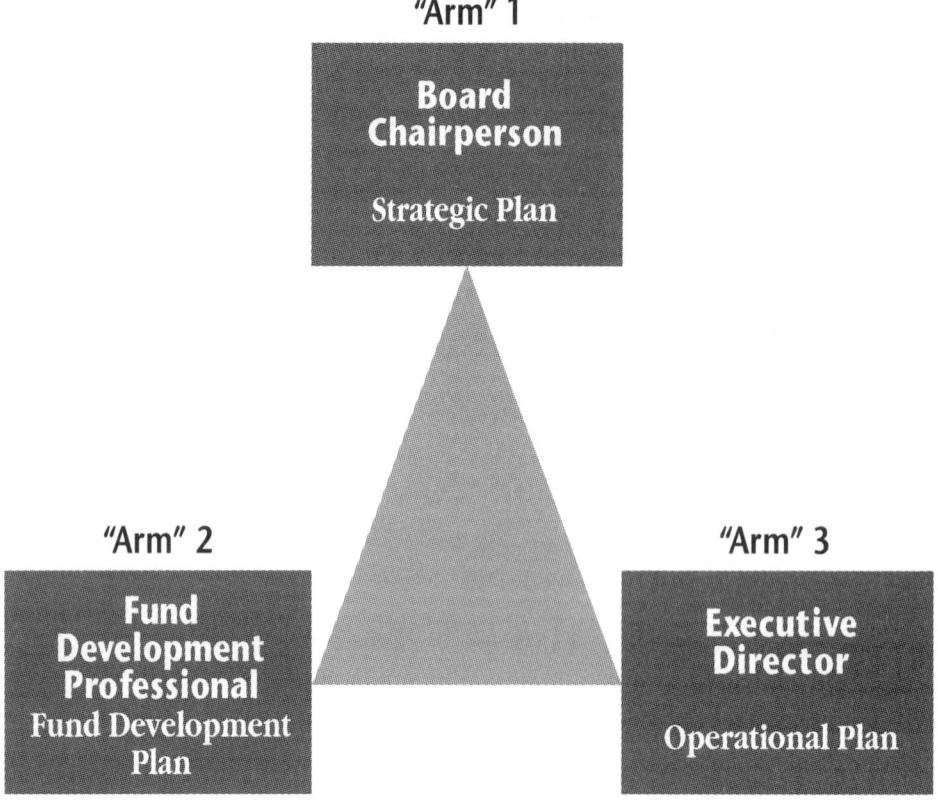

At the center of a board development team are the leaders of an organization's three key "arms." These individuals, who supervise the organization's three long-range plans, include: the board president, who oversees the strategic plan; the executive director, who manages the day-to-day operational plan; and the fund development professional, who is responsible for the fund development plan.

THE BOARD DEVELOPMENT TEAM

Full Team Composition

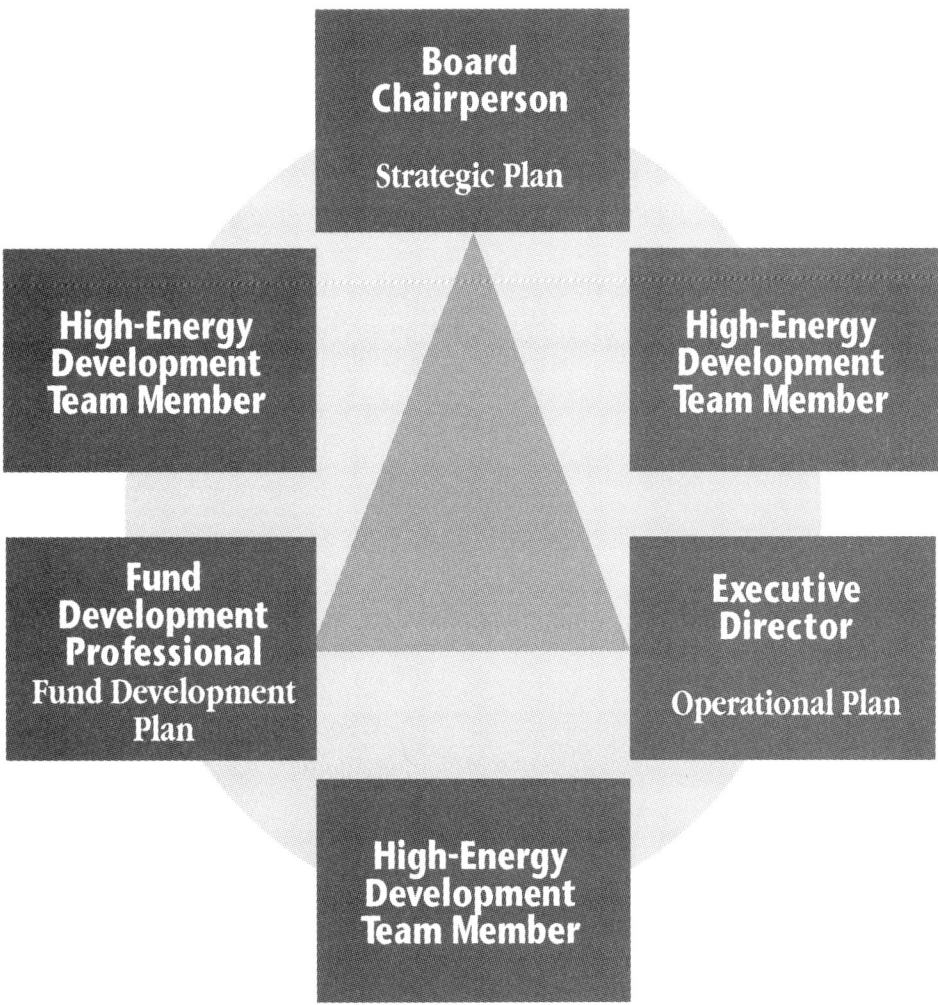

In addition to the three leaders who make up the development team "hub," there may be up to three additional members. These individuals should be high-profile, high-energy people who can help you connect with your "ideal" board prospects.

CHAPTER

Assess the Organization's Needs

Conduct a needs assessment 19
Step #1: Align the organization's goals 19
Why bring goals together? 19
Alignment is like a boat 20
How goal alignment is accomplished 20
Modify goals if necessary 21
Step #2: Inventory board members' skills 21
Matrix measures board members' skills 22
Using the assessment matrix 22
The board assessment process 23
Interpreting assessment results 23
Measuring staff needs 23
Step #3: Develop a recruiting strategy 24
Recruiting strategy thought process 24
Recruiting strategy provides short- and long-term benefits 25
Step #4: Prepare a formal action plan 26
Warning: Take your time developing the action plan 27
Report finalized action plan to the whole organization 27
Ongoing assessments keep recruiting strategy up-to-date 28
STOP! Procedure checkpoint 29
 Board Profile/Assessment Matrix (Table 1) 30
 Board Profile/Assessment Matrix (Table 2) 31
 Board Profile/Assessment Matrix (Table 3) 32
 Current Board Member Names 33
 Action Plan Template 34

CHAPTER

Assess the Organization's Needs

O nce in place, the board development team can begin the strategic recruiting process. Initially, this means conducting a top-to-bottom assessment of the organization's goals and its current board members. ■ This evaluation tells the board development team two things: what goals the organization wants to reach, and what skills the board needs to reach them. Development team members can then use this information to develop detailed profiles for the types of board members they want to recruit. ■ The assessment process is done in two phases: The first involves analyzing goals identified in the long-range, operational and fund development plans and evaluating all current board members and their skills. The second deals with merging this information into a recruiting strategy. ■ This chapter explains how the board development team should conduct each phase of the assessment. It also describes how team members should summarize the recruiting strategy in a formal action plan. ■

❏ ■ CONDUCT A NEEDS ASSESSMENT

As nonprofit executive director and leader of the board development team, it's essential that you stress the importance of this preliminary research step. Otherwise, the team risks rushing through the assessment and recruiting the wrong people.

For example, without adequate research you may overlook the need to recruit a planned giving expert—even though your organization is planning a capital campaign. Or you might recruit a public relations specialist, when you really need a marketing professional who can sell the nonprofit's services.

When this happens, you have a board with excellent skills, but not necessarily the skills to help the organization reach its goals.

To identify the right people for your board, follow this four-step assessment and planning process:

■ Align the goals of the strategic plan, operating plan and fund development plan

■ Determine the board's skills and connections

■ Develop a recruiting strategy

■ Summarize the organization's goals and recruiting strategy in an action plan

Each of these steps will move you closer to the goal of having a high-profile board that gets things done. Here are the specifics…

❏ ■ STEP #1: ALIGN THE ORGANIZATION'S GOALS

Before the board development team can move forward, it must have a clear picture of the organization's goals. Development teams build this picture by reviewing the three "goal plans" nonprofits should have in place:

■ **Long-range/strategic plan.** This plan is written and approved by the board. It usually spans three to five years and outlines in general terms what the organization wants to achieve and how to do it.

■ **Operational plan.** The executive director writes this plan. It includes the day-to-day budget that shows how the organization works, and contains expense allocations and plans for future expansions. Operational plans are shorter than strategic plans and often cover a period of one year or less.

■ **Fund development plan.** This plan describes how the organization will raise money in coming years, as well as the amount of revenue anticipated from each fund raiser. Its length is usually from one to three years. It may be longer, however, if capital improvements are involved.

Why bring goals together?

The purpose of bringing these three goal plans together is twofold:

First, and most important, goal alignment guides the board development team in identifying recruitment needs. For example, if goals clearly show that a lot of money needs to be raised in the next two years, the team can make recruiting a major gifts fund raiser its top priority.

Second, aligning goals helps nonprofit departments share resources and improve overall efficiency.

In some organizations, for example, departments operate independently of one another. The fund development office raises money, the executive director and program supervisors oversee services, and the board establishes policy and sets long-range goals. While there is some intercommunication, rarely do the three collaborate and use a single contact for multiple purposes. As a result, several members of the same organization may unknowingly repeat contact with the same individual or organization.

The goal alignment process breaks through this communication barrier. It forces each arm of the nonprofit to outline for the others what it's trying to do and how it's doing it. As a result, each has a better understanding of how the others work—and how they can help one another.

Alignment is like a boat

A well-practiced rowing team is a good analogy to describe the effects of goal alignment. Think of your nonprofit as the boat. The fund development director, the executive director and the board chairperson are the people in it.

Everyone in the boat is rowing in the same direction—but not at the same time. Under these circumstances, progress will be either painstakingly slow, or the boat will be moving in circles. If the group coordinates its efforts and rows in the same direction at the same time, progress will be quicker and smoother.

That is what happens when the board development team aligns the organization's goals. It finds out how the three arms of the nonprofit can cooperate to make quicker progress toward the ultimate goal—providing more and better programs to the people you serve.

How goal alignment is accomplished

The process of aligning plans will generally take from two to three meetings of about two hours each.

During these meetings, each key player on the board development team—the board chairperson, the executive director and the fund development professional—takes a turn presenting their respective plans. A discussion of what each one needs to do to reach individual goals, and how they can work together to accomplish them, follows.

Here's an example of how this process works...

The board chairperson states that, within five years, the organization wants to be able to serve 5,000 individuals in daytime programs and 2,000 in overnight programs. This goal is part of the strategic plan.

The executive director responds by explaining how this goal fits into the operational plan. Currently, the nonprofit is serving 3,000 in daytime programs and 1,000 in overnight programs, at a cost of $3 million.

To reach the goal, daytime programs must increase by 2,000 people and overnight programs by 1,000 people. This means three more facilities must be built or rented to provide space for the expanded programs. Fund development will have to raise these revenues, plus the additional costs of increasing staff and resources to run the programs.

The fund development professional then describes how this need will or won't fit into his or her department's goals.

For instance, the fund development department is in the middle of a campaign to increase the organization's endowment by $5 million. Staff is also trying to raise the remaining $2 million to maintain current programs, for a total of $7 million from the current donor base.

The fund development office points out that, at the current cost of $475 per person, it will have to raise an additional $2 million to cover program expansions and staff additions. Several million more dollars will be needed to pay for the additional facilities needed to provide expanded services. To do this, the fund development office asks for larger contributions from board members and their help in growing the nonprofit's donor prospect list.

Modify goals if necessary

Occasionally, some goals may have to be changed in order to be fully aligned. In the example cited, it may be impossible for the fund development department to raise enough money to meet the strategic plan's goal.

In that case, the strategic goal may have to be pared back, or the fund development department may have to change some of its goals.

For example, it may decide to add only $2 million to the endowment fund—instead of the planned $5 million—so an additional $3 million is available to pay for increased services.

❏ STEP #2: INVENTORY BOARD MEMBERS' SKILLS

You should look at your organization the same way the manager of a baseball team looks at his players. Your goal is to win games. To do this, you watch your players, determine which positions need improvement and then bring in different players with the skills to get the job done.

You should analyze your organization's board with one eye constantly on areas for improvement, and then act accordingly.

Identifying these areas is the board development team's next step in this assessment process. After the team has aligned the nonprofit's goals, it must look closely at current board members' skills and expertise. Do they have what it takes to lead a winning and growing organization? If not, what skills are missing?

Matrix measures board members' skills

To identify specific skills that need improvement—or skills that must be added altogether—development team members should complete a Board Profile/Assessment Matrix. A sample is on Pages 30-32.

A Board Profile/Assessment Matrix is a simple tool that shows the current board's skill strengths and deficiencies in a way that's easy for the development team to understand. Since it's anonymous, it also safeguards board members' confidentiality.

The sample assessment matrix in this manual has three parts:

The first, Table #1, on Page 30, is used to inventory current board members according to areas of expertise and professional skills. For example, development team members identify whether each board member has background in areas like human resources, finance, public relations and strategic planning.

This table also identifies the levels of board member participation. It asks if individual board members have served on committees and/or as board officers.

Table #2, the second part of the assessment, is similar to Table #1—except that it breaks down the board demographically.

For example, it identifies the average age of board members, their gender and their ethnic background. This is especially valuable information for boards that want to diversify their membership.

Assessment categories from both tables can be "mixed and matched" as needed. Or board development teams can build their own matrices. For instance, if the category of "religious expertise" is irrelevant to your nonprofit, simply cross it off the list.

You're also welcome to add categories to the list. The category "arts and entertainment" isn't part of the ready-made list of "Areas of Expertise/Professional Skills." If this is important to your organization's board, add it to the matrix. (Use the blank assessment matrix on Page 32 to build a customized version of the ready-made matrices.)

The third part of this assessment tool, found on Page 33, is a blank list for board member names. This is where the development team should begin its evaluation.

Using the assessment matrix

Beginning on the first line of the Board Member Names form, fill in the names of your organization's board members. Each person should be listed on a separate line. Then turn back to the evaluation matrix.

Across the top of the matrix is a row of numbers, 1 through 25. Those numbers correspond with board member names, according to the list you just completed. For example, if Jane Smith is number 12 on your list, she is Board Member #12 on the matrix.

Then for each board member, go down the "Areas of Expertise/Professional Skills" column and place a check in the column of each individual who has a particular skill. For instance, if Jane Smith (Board Member #12) is an attorney, check the box in column #8 beside the "Legal" category.

Be careful, however, not to credit an individual with a skill that he or she isn't proficient in. Members should receive checks in the skills categories that they most obviously bring to the board.

For example, a public relations

professional would receive a mark in that particular category because it's his or her primary skill. This same person probably shouldn't receive a mark in the fund development category for community awareness work he or she did for two or three campaigns some years ago. The work isn't recent, and it isn't significant enough to make this individual an "expert" on fund development.

Editor's Note: The separate list of board member names is designed to maintain as much confidentiality as possible. This anonymity also makes it possible to include a copy of the assessment results in a report to the full board. (More about the development team's reporting responsibility is in Chapter 7.)

The board assessment process

The assessment process is completed in two phases—at an individual level, then at a team level.

Each board development team member should complete an assessment of his or her board peers. Later, team members can discuss the assessment's results and come to consensus about who deserves credit for which skills, as well as which skills the current board lacks.

This step in the assessment process is relatively short. If team members do the assessment on their time, comparing results and reaching consensus at a meeting should take no more than two hours.

Interpreting assessment results

As team members work through the assessment matrix, it will be obvious where the gaps

are. Skill lines with no check marks on them will stick out like the proverbial sore thumb.

These are areas in which your board is weak. The board development team should concentrate on them when formulating its overall recruiting strategy. For example, if no current board member has marketing expertise, this is a skill you should look for in prospective board candidates.

Just as you did in the goal alignment process, summarize the findings of this assessment in a memo to the full board. You also may include a copy of the assessment matrix to illustrate needs outlined in writing.

Measuring staff needs

As your organization grows and moves toward its goals, its staff will grow and change as well.

Staff assessment and growth are left to the discretion of the executive director. He or she should make provisions in the operational plan for additional staff training or more stringent hiring criteria (for example, applicants must have a college degree instead of a high school diploma) necessary to meet the organization's goals.

On the other hand, the board development team shouldn't be completely in the dark about these changes.

The executive director should report all staff needs—like creating or eliminating full- and/or part-time positions—to the board development team. This keeps the board chairperson and fund development professional in tune with operational changes. It also ensures that goals remain aligned, and that the board stays on target to attain them.

❏ STEP #3: DEVELOP A RECRUITING STRATEGY

Now that the nonprofit's goals are aligned and the skills of the board have been assessed, the board development team is ready to start thinking about the actual business of recruiting. And it will begin by using aligned goals and the Profile/Assessment results to develop a formal recruiting strategy.

A recruiting strategy is the board development team's game plan. It spells out what the team is going to do and why. Specifically, a recruiting strategy includes:

■ the organization's aligned goals

■ the board's strengths and weaknesses

■ the number of anticipated board vacancies

■ the kind of people the board development team would like to recruit to fill them

■ where it plans to find qualified candidates

Recruiting strategy thought process

As stated earlier, the purpose of this initial research—goal alignment and the Board Profile/Assessment—is to help you recruit the right people. So far, though, you've only been collecting information.

Developing a recruiting strategy is your first opportunity to apply what you've learned to recruiting. Here's a scenario that illustrates how this transition is made…

Step #1) Review the nonprofit's goals. Let's assume that Nonprofit XYZ's board development team aligned the organization's goals and agreed that increasing its programs by 25% over two years was a top priority.

To reach this goal, the team realized the board and fund development department needed to rejuvenate the nonprofit's public image—and raise 20% more revenue than originally planned. This meant increasing fund raising efforts and launching a marketing campaign.

Step #2) Review the Board Profile/ Assessment results. After assessing current board members' skills, the XYZ development team finds significant weaknesses in the areas of fund raising and legal issues. It also sees that the board's marketing know-how isn't as strong as it thought—only two of 12 members have professional experience in this area, and one of them is about to rotate off the board.

Step #3) Know the number of board vacancies. The Profile/Assessment Matrix asks development team members to state when each board member's term expires. This lets team members know at a glance how many positions they must recruit for.

In the case of our hypothetical Nonprofit XYZ, the number of openings was three.

Step #4) Realize that vacancies mean the loss of skills. When members leave the board, it loses those individuals' expertise. These skills must be replaced if they directly affect your board's ability to reach its goals.

One of Nonprofit XYZ's departing board members, for example, is a marketing professional. This is expertise that its development team needs to replace—especially since the organization is planning a growth phase that requires a new marketing campaign.

Step #5) Decide what type of people you need. This is where you begin combining the information you've gathered in Steps 1 through 3 to create a recruiting strategy.

This is accomplished by comparing the skills that your board currently has with the skills you'll need to reach the organization's goals.

For example, the board development team of Nonprofit XYZ knows that the organization needs to raise money to expand programs. The Profile/Assessment shows the team that board members probably don't have enough fund raising savvy to meet the goal. The team also realized that the board was about to lose one of its few members who have marketing experience—just when it needed to develop a new marketing campaign to accompany the fund drive.

To be successful, the board development team obviously needs to fill these skill gaps. So the team decides that at least two of the three new board members should have strong fund development backgrounds. This will help the board raise the additional money necessary for nonprofit growth.

The team also agrees to recruit an accomplished marketing specialist who can supervise and launch a communitywide campaign. This not only replaces the marketing expertise the board will lose through attrition, it will improve the current marketing skill level.

Step #6) Find a starting point. After the development team decides what type of individuals to recruit, it needs to make a list of places where it plans to find qualified candidates.

For instance, marketing professionals can be identified through the local chapter of the American Marketing Association. Or the development team may plan to call leading marketing firms in the area to ask for names of individuals who fit the board member profile. (More about board candidate sources is in Chapter 5.)

The board development team of Nonprofit XYZ, needing two strong fund raisers, decides to contact the local chapter of the National Society of Fund Raising Executives to obtain referrals. The team plans the same strategy with a chapter of the American Marketing Association.

Recruiting strategy provides short- and long-term benefits

A recruiting strategy doesn't just help the board development team get organized and focus on finding the right people. It also provides these short- and long-term benefits:

■ **A strategy identifies groups of people you truly need.** Instead of randomly asking friends and acquaintances to join the board—as some nominating committee members do—a recruiting strategy forces the development team to zero in on specific types of people. As a result, members recruit only individuals who have skills to improve the board.

■ **A strategy makes reshaping a board easier.** All boards change over time. They add and subtract members, and rewrite their bylaws. Sometimes, though, the actual direction of a board will change—e.g., moving from a first-generation, hands-on board to a more mature, second-generation governance board.

A recruiting strategy makes these board transition periods smoother.

For example, if your organization's goal is to reduce the number of board members, your recruiting strategy should outline how this will happen. It may state that your development team plans to replace only one of every three members who rotate off the board. To replace the skills of previous board members, your recruiting targets will be individuals with a whole package of skills.

This eases the transition between the old board and the new one because you've planned how to make the change. Everyone knows how the number of full board members will be reduced, which minimizes any "who will be the next to go" fear among members. Plus, the recruiting strategy has identified the specific skills the development team will look for in recruits—so the board is never without valuable expertise.

Both of these problems could surprise you if you don't plan for the changes—and arbitrarily cut the current membership.

■ **A strategy sets the stage for improving the overall quality of the board.** An ongoing part of every recruiting strategy should be to increase the caliber of board members—that is, to continually recruit individuals who are better-known and more accomplished than current members.

A recruiting strategy starts this process by identifying candidate sources outside the traditional circle of friends. Typically, these are groups of people more qualified for board positions than friends, colleagues and acquaintances.

After one high-profile candidate comes aboard, the strategy then demands that you find a second, third and fourth board member who matches this first person in accomplishments. The board ultimately will fill up with these higher-profile individuals. When this happens, the recruiting strategy starts over—and you start recruiting at the next level above these members. Over time, this will improve your board tremendously.

❏ STEP #4: PREPARE A FORMAL ACTION PLAN

The final step in the assessment process is writing and presenting an action plan that describes how the board development team intends to proceed. All action plans should be based on these three items:

■ **A statement of long-range goals.** This identifies specifically what the nonprofit hopes to accomplish and how the board will be structured.

■ **A clear recruiting strategy.** Well-conceived recruiting strategies outline the number and/or type of board vacancies you need to fill, skills the board needs to reach its goals, kinds of candidates the development team is looking for and places qualified candidates can be found.

The strategy should include the research results that led the development team to conclude as it did. For example, explain that team members will be searching for prospects with a strategic planning background because the Profile/Assessment showed that no current board members have expertise in this area— and the organization needs to develop a new five-year plan for the future.

■ **A time-line.** Spelling out expectations for the board development team puts some accountability pressure on its members. Because team members know that the full board expects specific actions by certain dates, they're more likely to follow through with commitments and stay on schedule with the plan.

The time-line should provide clear checkpoints for the development team. For example, a time-line might state that, "Within three months of today, 10 prospects will be in the recruiting and evaluation process." Time-lines may also specify a minimum number of initial contacts to be made and a date those should be completed.

Editor's Note: An Action Plan Template is on Pages 34-35.

Warning: Take your time developing the action plan

Your organization's action plan won't be written in a day—or even a month.

On average, it requires two to four meetings of the board development team, each at least one and one-half hours in length, to go through this evaluation process. The first meeting, and possibly the second, are devoted to aligning goals. At the following meetings, development team members complete the Board Profile/Assessment Matrix, develop a recruiting strategy and write an action plan.

Don't be surprised if the process takes longer than two to four meetings. For many organizations, the initial meeting of the board development team is the first time all three plans—strategic, operational and fund development—have ever been brought together and discussed. This lengthens the review and alignment process significantly.

It's important to remember, however, not to rush through this evaluation stage. The quality of work done now will pay off as the recruiting process progresses.

Report finalized action plan to the whole organization

When the board development team finalizes the action plan, it will have taken a giant step toward improving board member recruitment procedures, as well as the board itself.

Development team members will also have spent a great deal of time working together and communicating with the full board through memos. Now, however, is the best time for the team to unveil its complete action plan to all board and nonprofit staff members.

This presentation, like the action plan itself, should touch on everything the development team has done to this point. Goals laid out in the strategic plan, the operational plan and the fund development plan should be reiterated, and the alignment process explained.

For example, use copies of the aligned goals and the Board Profile/Assessment Matrix to show board and staff members what the nonprofit's needs are. Then describe the kind of candidates you're looking for, where you're going to find them and the professional recruitment process. In other words, talk them through your recruiting strategy step by step.

This alerts board members to the team's plans and gives them a chance to ask questions about the recruiting process. The action plan also lets them know what type of individuals or resources from their own networks they might recommend to the development team.

To make the actual presentation, your board development team should use this two-pronged approach...

Step #1) Present the plan to the whole board. No special meeting of the board is necessary for this presentation. Simply present the action plan during a regularly scheduled board meeting.

The development team captain, usually the executive director, may lead the presentation for the group. The team captain, however, doesn't have to explain the entire plan to board members. The presentation may be divided among other development team members and given in segments. This conveys to board members that the entire team is involved and committed and supports the plan.

Step #2) Update staff members on the development team's activities and plans. The formation of the board development team and restructuring of the recruiting process are major changes in how the board works. This often requires a change in board bylaws—a change that the nonprofit's staff should be informed about.

The best way to let staff members know what's going on is to distribute copies of the minutes from the board meeting when the development team presented its action plan. This way, staff members hear everything that board members heard.

Then, to clarify the meeting minutes, hold a staff meeting and review the plan with staff members face to face. This gives them a chance to ask questions and to hear firsthand what the board is doing to help the organization reach its goals.

Ongoing assessments keep recruiting strategy up-to-date

At the beginning of this chapter, this evaluation process was referred to as an "initial" assessment. That's because assessment should be an ongoing task—not something that's done only once every two or three years.

The board development team should constantly reassess the organization's position. In fact, every time the nonprofit reaches a goal or sets a new one, the executive director, board chairperson and fund development professional should align their plans and arrange to share resources as needed.

A complete assessment should be an annual event. This ensures that the board member recruiting strategy is up-to-date and that board development team members continue recruiting prospects and building a candidate pool with individuals who can help the nonprofit attain its goals. ■

STOP! Procedure checkpoint

Before moving on to Step 3 of the strategic recruiting process, Develop Board Position Profiles, have you...

❑ Met with the board development team to align the goals in your organization's long-range, operational and fund development plans?

❑ Summarized the aligned goals?

❑ Developed a customized Board Profile/Assessment Matrix?

❑ Inventoried board members' skills using this matrix?

❑ Summarized the board skills assessment findings?

❑ Developed and summarized a recruiting strategy?

❑ Written a formal action plan that includes a statement of the organization's goals, the development team's recruiting strategy and a time-line for completion?

❑ Presented the action plan to the full board?

❑ Presented the action plan to all staff members?

BOARD PROFILE/ASSESSMENT MATRIX

Table 1: Skills

Area of Expertise/ Professional Skills	Current Board Members																									New Board Candidates					
	1	2	3	4	5	6	7	8	9	10	11	12	13	14	15	16	17	18	19	20	21	22	23	24	25	A	B	C	D	E	F
Administrator																															
Architect																															
Business/Corporate																															
Community Leader																															
Educator																															
Executive Director																															
Finance																															
Accounting																															
Banking & Trust																															
Investments																															
Foundation Representative																															
Fund-raising																															
Government Representative																															
Human Resources																															
Insurance																															
Legal																															
Marketing																															
Media																															
Medical																															
Public Relations																															
Real Estate																															
Recruiting																															
Religious																															
Strategic Planning																															
Special Program																															
Board Officers/Committees																															
President																															
Vice Chair																															
Treasurer																															
Secretary																															
Board Development																															
Executive																															
Finance																															
Fund Development																															
Marketing																															
Planning																															

The forms on Pages 30-33 are Adapted from *Six Keys to Recruiting, Orienting and Involving Nonprofit Board Members,* by Judith Grummon Nelson. Published by National Center for Nonprofit Boards. For more information, call (202)452-6262. Used with permission.

BOARD PROFILE/ASSESSMENT MATRIX

Table 2: Demographics

Area of Expertise/ Professional Skills	Current Board Members																									New Board Candidates					
	1	2	3	4	5	6	7	8	9	10	11	12	13	14	15	16	17	18	19	20	21	22	23	24	25	A	B	C	D	E	F
Age																															
Under 35																															
From 36 to 50																															
From 51 to 65																															
Over 65																															
Gender																															
Women																															
Men																															
Race/ethnic background																															
Asian																															
Afro American																															
Hispanic/Latino																															
Native American																															
Caucasian																															
Other																															
Geographic location																															
City																															
Suburbs																															
State																															
Country																															
Contribution Inkind (I)																															
Donation (D) Solicited (S)																															
>10K																															
2-10K																															
2-5K																															
1-2K																															
<1K																															
Length of board service																															
Over 10 years																															
5 to 10 years																															
2 to 4 years																															
Less than 2 years																															
None																															
Attendance																															
75-100%																															
50-74%																															
25-49%																															
<24%																															
Term of expiration																															

BOARD PROFILE/ASSESSMENT MATRIX

Table 3: Create Your Own

Area of expertise and/or other evaluation criteria	Current Board Members (by number)																				Candidates				
	1	2	3	4	5	6	7	8	9	10	11	12	13	14	15	16	17	18	19	20	A	B	C	D	E

CURRENT BOARD MEMBER NAMES

Current Board Members

1. _____
2. _____
3. _____
4. _____
5. _____
6. _____
7. _____
8. _____
9. _____
10. _____
11. _____
12. _____
13. _____
14. _____
15. _____
16. _____
17. _____
18. _____
19. _____
20. _____

Board Member Candidates

A. _____
B. _____
C. _____
D. _____
E. _____

ACTION PLAN TEMPLATE

After completing the goal alignment process and board member assessment, identify the two most critical open positions on your board. Then complete this form, which specifies who will be responsible for which tasks, and when they should be completed.

POSITION #1: _____

WHO is responsible	WHAT is the task	WHEN will it be done	OUTCOMES expected from it

POSITION #2: _____

WHO is responsible	WHAT is the task	WHEN will it be done	OUTCOMES expected from it

CHAPTER

Develop Board Position Profiles

Position profile structure **41**
Assessment results and goals provide a starting point 41
Key positions help build your board 41
Content of position profiles 42
Element #1: Scope 42
Element #2: Experience and skills 42
Element #3: Key duties and responsibilities 42
Element #4: Expectations 43
Element #5: Key priorities 43
Profile development process **44**
Begin profile development with brainstorming sessions 44
Computer simplifies writing process 45
Position profiles yield future benefits 45
Profiles guide board referrals 46
STOP! Procedure checkpoint 47
    Position Profile Template 48
    Sample Position Profile 50

CHAPTER

Develop Board Position Profiles

When recruiting board members and volunteers, keep this question in mind: How do you know if you've found it if you don't know what it is you're looking for? ■ If you know what type of people—and skills—will benefit your organization, you can go into the community and find them. What you first need is a clear outline of what you're looking for. ■ Unfortunately, some nonprofit boards don't identify the qualities of an ideal candidate before starting the search for new members. They simply go to their circle of friends and find someone—anyone—who's willing to serve. Little, if any, attention is given to the skills their boards need, or how the candidates fit with the goals of the nonprofit. ■ It's time to take the third step in the strategic recruiting process: writing position profiles for board vacancies. These documents provide an outline of the ideal board member candidate—so you'll know when you've found what you're looking for. ■

❑ POSITION PROFILE STRUCTURE

Position profiles are written descriptions of board members' individual roles and responsibilities. Each board position has its own profile. Position profiles are similar to job descriptions for staff members—only they're used a bit differently.

Like job descriptions, profiles define the board "job" and identify its specific duties, expectations and responsibilities. Profiles also outline the experience and skills that candidates need to meet these commitments. The development team uses position profiles to identify candidates with appropriate skills and to determine which of them is best suited for the position—just like a supervisor hiring a new staff member does.

Job descriptions usually remain constant over time. Position profiles are much more flexible, however, and can be changed to fit the plans and needs of your organization.

For example, let's say that your board currently needs a high-profile fund raiser to help with an upcoming capital campaign. So you make fund raising expertise and experience a key part of the position profile.

Later, when this board member resigns, you'll rewrite the position profile to match your organization's new needs. By then, public relations may have replaced fund raising as your top priority.

Assessment results and goals provide a starting point

Eventually, all board positions will have position profiles. As a start, though, the board

development team should create profiles for only one or two key board positions. Profiles for the remaining positions can be written later.

To decide which position profiles to write first, think about the development team's assessment of the nonprofit and its recruiting strategy. What are the immediate goals of the organization? What skills are needed to accomplish these goals? What expertise does the board lack?

If fund raising is a major concern, write one of the position profiles to fit your ideal fund development committee chairperson. Or if establishing contact with local or state government is a priority, write a profile that focuses on this type of background.

Remember, though, your decision should be based on both the board's skill needs and the organization's goals. Don't recruit an architect or an insurance expert simply because your board doesn't have one. Every position profile you write should describe a person who will help your nonprofit improve its services and meet its goals.

Key positions help build your board

If your board could benefit from stronger leadership, here's a suggestion for choosing the first positions to recruit for: Seek new talent for the fund development committee chairperson and the marketing committee chairperson positions.

These two positions are key to the organization's success. A financial expert can help your nonprofit build its resources, and a strong marketing campaign can help establish the nonprofit's presence in a competitive marketplace. Together, these elements set the stage for improved and expanded services, long-term financial stability and stronger community support.

Writing profiles for these two positions doesn't mean that you should immediately remove those who currently chair the fund development and marketing committees. They should serve out their terms. New recruits should be placed on the committees as regular members. Then when the current chairperson rotates out of that position, the individual recruited for that role can succeed him or her.

This gradual assimilation process helps maintain peace and continuity on affected committees, which helps garner the support of the current committee leadership. At the same time, new recruits to your nonprofit have a chance to familiarize themselves with committee issues and projects before assuming leadership positions.

Content of position profiles

What should be in a position profile?

A position profile is a one- to two-page summary of the qualifications and requirements of a board "job." (A sample Position Profile Template is on Pages 48-49.) It tells board candidates everything they need to know about what's expected of them should they choose to become a full member.

The typical profile should begin by identifying the specific position. This is followed by the five categories that all profiles include...

Element #1: Scope

This is a single statement that explains in general terms what the job is and what you expect from those filling it. A sample scope statement might read:

"To establish a community relations campaign that increases public awareness of the upcoming capital campaign."

Element #2: Experience and skills

In the Experience and Skills portion of the profile, write the minimum background a candidate must have to be qualified for the position.

For example, if you're looking for a chairperson for the fund development committee, one requirement could be three years of board experience as chair of a capital and major gifts campaign. For a marketing specialist, the minimum background may be an individual who heads his or her own consulting firm and who has more than 10 years of experience in managing direct sales and multimedia campaigns.

Element #3: Key duties and responsibilities

This section of the profile is most like a job description. It lists everything a person in the board position is responsible for.

For example, the marketing committee chairperson's duties may include something like, "Will develop key marketing strategies, recruit committee members and supervise a direct mail campaign."

Element #4: Expectations

In this portion of the position profile, clearly state what you expect from the prospective board member—and don't pull any punches!

Specific requirements, tasks, goals and performance objectives should be stated in measurable terms. It is helpful to think in terms of Who, What, When, Where and How.

Highly qualified board candidates are busy people who want—and need—to know what a commitment entails. They need to know that what's expected of them is also something they're able to do. By leaving information off the profile, you're being unfair to yourself and the prospect.

It's unfair to you because you risk not getting the performance from the board member that you need. For example, if you only tell a prospect that he or she must make a personal contribution to the organization, you may have someone join the board and give $1,000—when you really needed $2,500 or more.

And it's unfair to the prospect because he or she commits to the board expecting to do certain things. If you spring new responsibilities on him or her, that individual may not be able—or willing—to follow through.

If prospective board members turn you down because they can't meet your expectations, you should feel good about the requirements you've laid out. The profile is working. It's finding prospects who can do what needs to be done and weeding out the candidates who can't or won't commit 100% to the projects you're working on.

You may find, too, that some candidates are willing to commit for a lesser amount of time, money or service. This information can help you make arrangements that will accommodate the willingness to serve at this level and your organization's needs.

Element #5: Key priorities

In addition to the personal skills, experience and expectations already outlined, position profiles include a brief summary of the organization's priorities.

On the Position Profile Template, these priorities are communicated by a checklist. The board development team ranks each area on a scale of 1 to 10, according to its overall importance. For example, if establishing a major gifts campaign or capital campaign is a key priority, then the categories of high profile—contacts, clout and wealth—will be ranked 10.

Your board development team should discuss each priority separately, then come to consensus on its ranking. The form also provides a space for the development team to identify special assignments the prospective board member will be involved with.

The ranking-style format of these priorities allows flexibility—as organization priorities change, their rankings can change as well.

Editor's Note: Following the Position Profile Template which is on Pages 48-49 is a completed sample profile. Feel free to use it as a model while completing position profiles for your own board.

❑ PROFILE DEVELOPMENT PROCESS

Developing position profiles often takes several hours, so schedule a board development team meeting just for this purpose. Best results are achieved when members aren't distracted by other team-related business—like assessments or aligning goals—or worried about meetings extending late into the evening.

Begin profile development with brainstorming sessions

Here's the development process you should follow:

Step 1) Think about your organization's goals and action plan. As you prepare to write the profile for a specific board position, think about the role this member plays in your nonprofit, and how that role may need to change for the organization to reach its goals.

What specific skills have past chairpersons of the marketing committee lacked? How did that affect the committee's productivity? How will future marketing committee chairpersons be involved in future plans? What skills will they need to be successful?

You can save time on this step by giving development team members advance notice of which position profiles will be discussed. This gives them time to think about the job and prepare notes for the meeting.

Step 2) Open discussion with a brainstorming session. Ask development team members, "What does the title 'Marketing Committee Chairperson' bring to mind?"

Get started by throwing ideas on the table. Don't worry about where—or if—they fit into the finished product. Just speak off the top of your head and let your peers' ideas stimulate your own thinking.

Step 3) Organize random thoughts to fit the Position Profile Template. After you've generated as much information as possible about a specific position, separate the ideas into their appropriate categories. For example, decide which thoughts fall under "Duties and Responsibilities" and which are more accurately labeled "Expectations."

Step 4) Fill in any gaps in individual categories. As the categories are filled, you may think of additional items. Add them to the profile.

Step 5) Edit from general ideas to specific requirements. Now the real work begins! The general ideas currently in the profile template must be shaped into very specific statements that tell board members what they're supposed to do.

A few words of warning are in order here: First, don't accept the first edit as the finished product. Every time team members go through the profile and tighten the statements, the stronger the profile becomes. A profile that's been edited six times will be clearer and more accurate than one that's been edited only twice. Continue editing until team members can't think of anything else to add, or a better way of phrasing something.

Second, be aware that the profile may actually grow in length during the editing process. Some general ideas may each break down into five or six more specific tasks—

which will increase overall length.

For example, a broad responsibility, like "Establish the nonprofit's presence in the marketplace," will break down into many smaller pieces. Among these may be "Redesign the organization's informational brochure so it appeals to all audiences," and "Create and supervise a marketing campaign to boost program participation."

Computer simplifies writing process

Many boards still use a chalkboard and eraser when they sit down to write out plans, goals and other board documents. Writing position profiles is much easier when a personal computer is part of the process!

Using a personal computer and printer eliminates someone having to write on the chalkboard. A computer also makes it easier for development team members to see how their revisions affect the finished product—as well as revisions that are still needed.

You can take advantage of this by arranging for someone with a computer and printer to be in the room while the team works its way through the writing and editing process. As changes are made, they can be entered into the computer, and updated versions of the profiles can be printed and distributed to team members.

This way, team members can make notes to themselves and hammer out the exact language with a pen and paper. There's no need for members to try remembering it all in their heads, or to rely on a group leader to organize everything on a chalkboard or flip-chart.

When the final draft is completed, copies of the profile should be printed for each member of the development team. A master copy should be maintained on computer diskette, as well as in hard-copy form.

Position profiles yield future benefits

Some executive directors may question why so much time and effort should be devoted to writing position profiles—especially when board members will rotate off the board and the process has to be done all over again.

Yes, writing position profiles is a lot of work. It's also an ongoing process. Position profiles, however, are an invaluable part of recruiting. Without them, your board would never realize these benefits…

■ **Profiles increase the likelihood that the candidates you recruit will fulfill your board's needs.** With a position profile in hand, you'll never be left hoping that the prospect you just talked to can learn the skills of a good fund development committee chairperson. He or she will already have them.

Thanks to the very clear qualifications outlined in the profile, the individuals you approach will have the expertise your development team is searching for. If the prospect didn't measure up to these standards, he or she wouldn't have been approached in the first place.

■ **Profiles keep all board development team members "on the same page."** Without profiles, team members are left on their own to decide what the vacant board position is about and what skills the ideal board member should have. And one team member's perception of the job doesn't necessarily match another member's perception.

Two things may happen as a result: First, team members may approach candidates who have widely disparate backgrounds—instead of candidates who have specific experience. For example, instead of finding board candidates with professional real-estate management experience, team members may recruit financial advisors and bankers.

Although these individuals may have experience similar to what you're looking for, they're not truly qualified for the job. If one of them joins the board, you'll still be left with a board member who has to learn by trial and error the skills of his or her position.

Second, different team members may contact the same candidate with different perceptions of the job. One team member will tell the prospect that the position includes responsibilities A, B and C. Another team member may tell the prospect something completely different. This leaves prospects feeling confused—and put off by your disorganization.

A position profile, however, ensures that all board development team members will be able to present an accurate, consistent picture of the board position, as well as recruit prospects with the skills you need.

■ **Profiles are good informational tools to use when making contacts.** When making an initial contact, reading from a position profile is an excellent way to describe the exact person you're searching for.

The profile's organization makes it easy to refer to, and it will help team members give consistent descriptions of the ideal candidate. Position profiles are also excellent informa-

tional pieces to leave with candidates after a personal meeting. (More about this is in Chapter 7, "Contact and Meet Candidate Prospects.")

Editor's Note: Because you'll be using copies of the profiles during the recruiting process, have them neatly typeset and photocopied. This can be done by the organization's staff using desktop publishing technology, or it can be professionally prepared at a print shop.

Taking this step ensures that your organization presents itself professionally.

■ **Profiles are the cornerstone of the evaluation and selection process.** Again, how will you know if someone isn't right for your nonprofit, if you don't know who is right?

Once you identify prospects, you can go back to this profile and ask if the person does, indeed, have the skills, experience and commitment to deserve a board position. If he or she is qualified, you can continue courting that individual through the recruiting process.

Profiles guide board referrals

After finalizing the position profiles, the board development team should share them with the full board. An effective way to do this is to distribute and discuss copies of the profiles at a board meeting.

Letting other board members know what kind of people you're looking for puts them in a position to help you. It also helps them feel as though they're playing a role in the recruitment process.

For example, if board members know individuals who meet the criteria listed in the profile, they can pass along their names. The board development team can then contact those people to talk with them about the board service opportunity. ▪

STOP! Procedure checkpoint

Before moving on to Step 4 of the strategic recruitment process, Script the Organization's Story, have you...

❑   Reviewed the purpose of a position profile with the board development team?

❑   Chosen one or two positions to write profiles for, based on the development team's assessment of the organization's needs and goals?

❑   Held a brainstorming session to develop the profiles?

❑   Edited the profiles until they define the positions exactly?

❑   Reached consensus among development team members that the profiles are finely tuned?

❑   Arranged for the profiles to be professionally typeset and photocopied?

❑   Shared the profiles and discussed ideal candidates with the full board?

POSITION PROFILE TEMPLATE

Position: _____

Organization: _____

Proposed term of service: _____

Scope of position

Experience/skills

Key duties/responsibilities

Expectations

Key priorities (Scale of 1 to 10, 10 being the highest)

_____ Leadership

_____ Governance

_____ Skills

_____ High profile

_____ Contacts

_____ Clout

_____ Wealth

_____ Special assignment (please specify): _____

_____ Fund raising; i.e.,

_____	Special events	_____	Major gifts
_____	Capital campaign	_____	Planned giving
_____	In-kind	_____	Annual campaign
_____	Donation	_____	Endowment
_____	Solicited	_____	Foundations
_____	Other (please specify): _____		

SAMPLE POSITION PROFILE

Position: Chairperson, Financial Development Committee

Organization: American Red Cross — Mid-American Chapter

Proposed term of service: 3 years

Scope of position

To significantly expand the capacity of the M.A.C./American Red Cross, to raise increasing amounts of financial support and to fund service and property strategies identified by the Board of Directors.

Experience/skills

■ Prior board leadership experience in a major institution raising at least $ _____ from annual operations and/or as chairperson of a capital endowment campaign of $ _____ over a five-year campaign period.

■ Ability to establish and maintain communication with persons of wealth and influence regarding their financial support of the organization.

Key duties/responsibilities

■ To lead the chapter's Annual Financial Development Campaign for three (3) fiscal years beginning _____ and ending _____ . The total campaign is $ _____ during fiscal year 1996 and increases a minimum of 7 percent each year.

■ To establish measurable key responsibilities, etc.

Expectations

■ Assist in the recruitment and selection of sub-committee chairpersons for the Financial Development Committee, i.e.,

- ❏ Direct response
- ❏ Major gifts
- ❏ Corporate foundations
- ❏ Annual dinner and other special events
- ❏ Planned giving

■ Indicate dates each sub-committee chairperson shall be in place.

■ Identify and recruit a qualified successor by July 1, 1997; train this successor during fiscal year 1996.

■ Participate in at least _____ board meetings and _____ committee meetings; attend annual meeting and other special events.

■ Make a three-year commitment to implement the fund development strategy.

■ Give/get pace-setting contribution(s) to the Annual Campaign of $ _____ or more.

■ Make $ _____ personal gift to the organization.

■ Ensure that donors of $ _____ or more are recognized at the benefactor table at the annual dinner.

Key priorities (Scale of 1 to 10, 10 being the highest)

__9__	Leadership
__6__	Governance
_____	Skills
__10__	High profile
__10__	Contacts
__9__	Clout
__9__	Wealth
_____	Special assignment (please specify): _____
_____	Fund raising; i.e.,

_____	Special events		_____	Major gifts
__10__	Capital campaign		_____	Planned giving
_____	In-kind		_____	Annual campaign
__7__	Donation		_____	Endowment
_____	Solicited		_____	Foundations
_____	Other (please specify): _____			

CHAPTER

Script the Organization's Story

Scripts provide information **57**
Elements of effective scripts 57
Element #1: Charter, mission, purpose 57
Element #2: Nonprofit services 57
Element #3: Current and future plans 58
Element #4: Expected outcomes 58
Element #5: The eight-step professional recruitment process 58
Write effective scripts **59**
Features and benefits encourage prospect involvement 60
Create an emotional hook 60
CASE STUDY: Emotional hook gets prospects involved 61
Tell prospects who's on the board too 61
Script format retains presentation flexibility 62
Script-writing procedure resembles profile-writing process 62
Benefits of script use **63**
CASE STUDY: Scripts give team members direction 64
STOP! Procedure checkpoint 65
　　Scripted Story Template 66
　　Features and Benefits Template 68
　　Sample Marketing Piece/Brochure 69

CHAPTER 4

Script the Organization's Story

So far in the strategic recruiting process, you've formed a board development team, assessed your organization's needs and developed position profiles that outline specific qualifications you're looking for in new board members. ■ Now you're ready to begin preparing to contact board member prospects. You need to decide what to say, how to say it in a way that makes serving on the board sound appealing, and in what order you're going to present it. ■ This process is called scripting the organization's story...

❑ SCRIPTS PROVIDE INFORMATION

Although this step in the strategic recruiting process is called scripting the organization's story, it's not a "script" per se. The document doesn't—and shouldn't—provide development team members with a word-for-word formula to use when talking to prospects.

Instead, a scripted story should organize team members' thoughts about the nonprofit organization.

A quality script gives the development team an outline to speak from when talking with board prospects. It helps members give strong, well-organized presentations—not rambling monologues put together off the tops of team members' heads, or stiff and obviously rehearsed lectures. Scripts allow development team members to be themselves, yet still be informative, well-structured and to the point in their conversation.

Scripts also may be used to develop sales/marketing brochures. After visiting potential board member sources and prospects, development team members can leave them a copy of the brochure to read at their leisure.

Elements of effective scripts

Scripts should present a clear picture of your organization and its goals. For best results, your script should have these five elements:
■ The charter, mission and purpose of the organization
■ Programs/services offered by the nonprofit
■ The organization's current and future plans

■ The expected outcome of your plans
■ The eight-step professional recruitment process

Element #1: Charter, mission, purpose

Of all elements in a scripted story, this is the easiest to put in words because it should already be part of the nonprofit's strategic plan.

A statement of charter, mission and purpose summarizes what the nonprofit is all about. It should state why the organization exists and what it hopes to accomplish through its programs and services.

If your organization doesn't already have a charter, mission and purpose statement in place, build one around these questions:
■ Why was this organization founded?
■ What is this nonprofit now trying to accomplish?
■ How do the organization's services benefit the community or constituents served?

Element #2: Nonprofit services

Following the organization's charter, mission and purpose is a description of its programs and services. This is where you discuss how the nonprofit fulfills its mission.

For example, if your nonprofit is a family shelter, you may state that one of its programs provides food, safety, counseling and legal advice to those who seek its help. As a result, troubled families are able to stay together and have a chance to get their lives back on track in a safe, supportive environment.

As you write your script, never assume that board prospects already know what your organization stands for. They may not be familiar with the nonprofit, or they may have incorrect information. All scripts should include a detailed description of the organization's services just for these situations. Team members may rarely need this information when meeting with board candidates, but these facts should be available nonetheless.

Element #3: Current and future plans

After you've outlined the organization's programs, explain how these services will be affected by your future plans. Specifically, review the goals of the strategic, operational and fund development plans. Include all capital improvements, like constructing a new building, and other plans—along with program expansions and fund raising campaigns.

This discussion of future plans lays the groundwork for why you need a particular candidate on the board. For example, he or she may be an architect or contractor with the know-how to monitor building construction. Or the prospect may be a fund raiser who can lead the capital campaign to pay for a major construction project.

Element #4: Expected outcomes

This part of the scripted story should stress how your plans will affect current programs and services. After hearing it, prospects should have an excellent idea of exactly how their skills will improve the quality of life for the people your organization serves and in the community as a whole.

If your plans include adding a new building, tell prospects that the expansion means you'll be able to increase services by 50% and add several new programs to meet community needs. A child services organization, for example, may be able to accommodate more children in its low-cost day-care programs. Or it may be able to start an after-school sports league for pre-teens and teenagers.

The ultimate outcome of this is that children and the community both benefit. The children are safer because more kids can be part of supervised activities when they're not with a parent. And because kids are in these activities, they're less likely to become part of other community-related problems.

Element #5: The eight-step professional recruitment process

This is a very straightforward part of the story. Before ending, simply summarize where the recruitment process goes next.

Most development teams tell prospects that other candidates are being interviewed and that all prospects are invited to attend nonprofit events, visit the facilities and meet the people served by the nonprofit's programs. Prospects who are interested in board service after subsequent visits with development team members may be invited to serve on a short-term board committee or team. Full governance board members are then chosen from this group of candidates.

You may think that the time and energy you put into discussing the recruitment process will serve little purpose. But explaining how your development team brings new members on board accomplishes three things:

■ **It shows prospects that the board is goal-oriented.** People recruited to serve on boards want to be part of an organization that knows how to get things done. Your strategic recruiting process—because it's so methodical—is a perfect way to show prospects that your board belongs in this category.

The strategic recruiting process shows prospects that your board has a clearly defined goal—a new board member with specific and accomplished skills. The research you've done, along with the recruiting steps you have yet to take, demonstrate that you have a plan for reaching this goal and that you'll accept nothing less than the best possible outcome.

When you don't discuss your recruitment process, however, you give candidates a much different impression. This leaves them thinking that you have no formal process for bringing people onto the board. Prospects may walk away believing that you'll take anyone who's interested, regardless of his or her skills or accomplishments.

This distinction is especially important to high-profile individuals. They want to know that you're making a commitment to use their skills, not just expecting them to attend meetings. Explaining the recruiting process, how your plans will improve the nonprofit's services and how the candidate's skills will be used to do this, conveys to candidates that you're serious about getting them involved—and serious about seeing some results.

■ **It puts candidates at ease.** Even if prospects have been recruited for other boards—and most high-profile candidates have—it's still a good idea to fill them in on your nonprofit's overall recruitment process. It puts them at ease knowing what will come next. It also assures them that neither you nor they will have to make a commitment after only one or two meetings or contacts.

■ **It distinguishes your nonprofit from others.** High-profile people are impressed by professionalism—and presenting them with a well-organized, highly selective recruiting process will leave prospects thinking: These people know what they're doing and I'm interested in learning more.

A non-professional, by-the-seat-of-your-pants recruiting approach puts off people who are already committed to many other things. Haphazard recruiting methods also bother prospects who are selective about the people they work with.

Editor's Note: A template for writing your own scripted story is on Pages 66-67.

❏ WRITE EFFECTIVE SCRIPTS

Each element of your script will have two parts—a features section and a benefits section. Structuring your script this way helps you tell and "sell" the board membership opportunity to prospects.

The first of these two parts is the nonprofit's features, or programs and services. Features are factual statements of what the organization does. Here's a sample feature statement: "The nonprofit provides preschool-aged child care and education programs from 6 a.m. until 9 p.m. daily."

Benefits are the corresponding results of the programs. They describe—in a less factual way—what the nonprofit's actions accomplish and what the effect of the feature is on the person receiving a service.

For example, a sample benefits statement may read, "Rather than being left in the care of a sibling or relative, or at a large child-care facility, children served by XYZ Nonprofit receive one-on-one care and are taught skills that better prepare them for school."

Features and benefits statements are easy to write and review if they're organized in a ledger-style format. The template for this should be arranged just like an accountant's ledger book. Instead of "Credits" and "Debits," however, the columns are labeled "Features" and "Benefits."

Editor's Note: A Features and Benefits Template is on Page 68.

Features and benefits encourage prospect involvement

Why should information be organized this way? Here's an example from the professional recruiting world to demonstrate...

As recruiters search for potential job candidates, they're approaching people who are already employed and obviously quite successful in their jobs. Most of the time, these people are content to stay where they are.

To get these individuals to consider a new opportunity, recruiters have to persuade them

that the position is worth exploring.

The most effective way to do this is to carefully present the features of the position—and then emphasize the benefits, or what's in it for the prospect. For instance, a recruiter could say, "You would have the personal satisfaction of dramatically increasing the quality of life for 1,000 learning-disabled children."

Recruiters who tell prospects only about the features of a position—like position description, compensation and employment benefits—would be moderately successful in getting them interested in the new position. Recruiters who concentrate on communicating the personal benefits of the position, however, get better results.

This "tell the features, sell the benefits" approach works because it taps into the prospect's emotional center. It appeals to his or her desire to tackle a challenge and do something important.

This tactic also works when recruiting nonprofit board members. To pique someone's interest in a position, stress how he or she would benefit from it. Unlike simple nuts-and-bolts information, this will motivate the prospect to learn more about the position and seriously consider your opportunity.

Create an emotional hook

Ideally, the "benefits statements" just discussed should also make an emotional appeal to the prospect's desire to help others.

This appeal shouldn't be so blatant that prospects feel that you're appealing to their sense of guilt. That type of approach will generate more contempt than support. You

CASE STUDY:
Emotional hook gets prospects involved

To illustrate the effectiveness of emotional hooks, consider this example:

I know of an organization representative who recently spoke to a large group about the programs the nonprofit offers to people infected with the HIV virus. The talk was about how these services could be expanded.

Several board members wanted to take the programs beyond service to those who already had HIV, and begin programs focused on prevention. Part of the service expansion was to launch a huge educational program.

The benefit of this was that future board members were going to be able to affect hundreds of thousands of youth in this particular location—simply by becoming part of the organization and maintaining this program. Since the program was aimed at prevention, they had an opportunity to touch the lives of more than 100,000 youths, and play a role in them not contracting the AIDS virus.

This group discovered that, at the heart and core of volunteers, there is a sense that if something feels good, then it's worthwhile. If there's satisfaction that the project is of great importance, that's where the appeal has to go. The response to this organization's appeal was positive because the illness was affecting large numbers of people in the area—and a prevention program was the only way to stop it.

should, however, clearly identify how your nonprofit solves a problem and then use phrases like, "We need your help and commitment to improve the quality of services provided."

This creates an emotional hook in prospects. The benefits statements help them empathize with your nonprofit's mission. Then by explaining how they can be a part of this mission, you draw them in even further.

Action: Train your board development team members to emphasize the "what's in it for me" aspect of board service when talking with prospects. Make sure they give an adequate explanation of why the prospect's skills are needed and how they will be used. Have team members spend the majority of time talking about how those skills will affect nonprofit programs and the people they serve.

Tell prospects who's on the board too

When talking to prospects, it helps to tell them who currently serves on your board and who are its key players.

This gives the prospect additional information on which to base his or her decision to learn more about serving on the board. After all, prospects want to know whom they will be working with. Identifying prominent individuals as board members is also enticing to prominent prospects.

If your board is in its early growth stages and currently has no members of significant stature in the community, you'll want to take a slightly different tack. Instead of telling prospects about the individuals they would be joining, present the board service opportunity as a chance to be part of a building process. Say to prospects, "We're trying to bring professionals like yourself onto the board, so we can improve the board's efficiency and the organization's programs. By joining the board, you'll not only serve the people who use our organization, you'll be participating in the organization's overall growth and improving its position in the marketplace."

Script format retains presentation flexibility

As you develop your script, remember that you're not writing a play. The goal isn't to provide dialogue—it's to provide team members an outline to speak from.

The argument against writing actual dialogue is simple: You can't predict how conversations will go.

A word-for-word script works only when meetings go as planned—and the prospect reacts exactly as anticipated. Then you can glide smoothly from one "line" to the next.

If something unexpected happens, however, the board development team has nothing to fall back on. Because the script doesn't have the flexibility to change with the conversation, team members won't know what to say next. This quickly turns confident presenters into disoriented ones—which can adversely affect the entire contact.

Having enough flexibility in the script to "roll with the punches" is essential. To create this, put the script's main ideas in a large-print, bullet-type layout. This format allows presenters to quickly glance at it, identify their next point and then speak casually about it. It's easy for speakers to follow, and the key words, phrases and statistics are easy to find when they're needed.

Script-writing procedure resembles profile-writing process

To write a script, the board development team should follow the same basic process used to write the position profiles.

As a group, brainstorm the elements of your organization's story. Then revise and edit your thoughts until you end up with a finished product.

This process is easiest if the team focuses on one element of the story at a time. For example, stick with the "benefits of future plans" section until you're done with it. Jumping between story elements makes organization difficult.

Start the process by choosing an element and listing its features. Then list the corresponding benefits. Edit and tighten the language until it says exactly what you want it to say. Move on to the next element only when you've finished the one you're currently working on.

For reference, keep copies of dictionaries and thesauruses on hand. They'll help you choose the proper words and stimulate brainstorming.

❏ BENEFITS OF SCRIPT USE

Some people believe that referring to notes during a presentation makes them look as though they don't understand what their organization does or why they're there. This mindset hurts more than it helps!

Using a script creates a favorable impression on prospects. It underscores the importance of the meeting and demonstrates personal organization, preparedness, a professional image and the desire to make a good impression. Scripts also result in these benefits…

Benefit #1) Scripts ensure consistency among team members' approaches. When board development team members begin contacting board prospects, it's very important that everyone gives these individuals the same basic information. This shows candidates that your nonprofit is organized and moving in a specific direction.

Without a uniform script, board development team members could easily end up looking confused. This gives the impression that each member has a different interpretation of key priorities.

Benefit #2) Scripts can be used to develop a leave-behind marketing piece. No matter how well you present your story at the sit-down meeting with board prospects, they won't be able to take everything in. They'll still want more information.

A well-prepared script can be used to develop an effective leave-behind marketing piece or brochure that you can give to the prospect. This way, the prospect can review the information at his or her leisure and make

a well-thought-out decision about becoming more involved—or recommending someone else to you.

Editor's Note: Like position profiles, your nonprofit's marketing piece should be professionally typeset and photocopied. This elevates the overall image of your board development team and organization.

A sample marketing piece is on Pages 69-74.

Benefit #3) Marketing pieces derived from scripts can be mailed or faxed to candidates after a telephone contact. If you call a prospect to present a board-service opportunity, one of the more common answers you'll receive is, "I'd like some more information before I make a decision."

This is why you meet personally with the individual. If that person doesn't want to schedule a meeting right away, or a convenient time isn't available in the near future, you can still accomplish this—by mailing or faxing a copy of your brochure/marketing piece.

This accomplishes two things: First, you provide the prospect with information he or she needs. Second, you get a head start on the meeting itself. Since the brochure will give the individual many of your nonprofit's vital statistics, you can focus less on the basics during your meeting. This means more time is available to discuss future goals and how that person can help you reach them.

Benefit #4) Marketing pieces or brochures can be mailed to third-party candidate sources. Sometimes, a prospect won't

CASE STUDY:
Scripts give team members direction

During a session I led at a professional conference, I walked a large organization through the initial stage of the script-writing process. The first step was to have the key personnel tell me—and the group in attendance—their organization's story.

I asked the board chairperson to go first. He was followed by the executive director, a finance officer and two key board members. Each had a different interpretation of the organization's priorities and needs regarding key board positions.

It's easy to see what effect this would have on board member recruitment. If a prospective candidate was approached by different board development team members and each team member had a different interpretation of needs and expectations of the prospect, the prospect—like the audience at the conference—would likely be confused. And as a result, the board prospect would probably not be interested in becoming part of a board that doesn't know what it's doing.

A scripted story, however, gives development team members a consistent platform to speak from. Each of them, no matter what his or her role in the organization, can present the same story. This shows candidates that the board is organized and focused on the future, which makes board service much more appealing.

be the person who eventually joins your board. He or she may be too busy to get involved or may not be interested.

This doesn't mean, however, that you should automatically end the call. These individuals may be willing to refer you to other people who would be better-suited to the job. (More about third-party referrals and leveraging contacts is in Chapter 6.)

To help these contacts make quality referrals, send them a copy of the brochure and position profiles. They can read about your organization and its goals, and then pass along the names of colleagues or acquaintances they feel can be of help. ■

STOP! Procedure checkpoint

Before moving on to Step 5 of the strategic recruiting process, Research Board Candidate Sources, have you...

❏ Reviewed the elements of an effective script?

❏ Gathered appropriate statistics and other information for the script?

❏ Met with development team members to write a script?

❏ Carefully edited all script elements so they clearly communicate your message?

❏ Included the recruitment process as part of the script?

❏ Used features and benefits to appeal to candidates' emotions?

❏ Prepared the script in a flexible, easy-to-read format?

❏ Arranged for the script to be professionally typeset and photocopied?

SCRIPTED STORY TEMPLATE

Organization name: _____

Year founded: _____

---------------------- CHARTER, MISSION AND PURPOSE ----------------------

---------------------- NONPROFIT PROGRAMS ----------------------

FUTURE PLANS

EXPECTED OUTCOMES

THE EIGHT-STEP PROFESSIONAL RECRUITMENT PROCESS

FEATURES AND BENEFITS TEMPLATE

Features of the organization	Benefits of the designated feature
■	
■	
■	
■	
■	
■	

SAMPLE MARKETING PIECE/BROCHURE

WHO WE ARE

Our Mission Statement

The American Red Cross is a humanitarian organization, led by volunteers, that provides relief to victims of disasters and helps people prevent, prepare for and respond to emergencies.

Our Work

The Mid-America Chapter is the local name for the American Red Cross in northeastern Illinois. We are one of a network of more than 1,900 Red Cross chapters nationwide, operating around the clock, every day of the year, providing these areas of service:

- community disaster relief
- safety and health education
- social services

The American Red Cross is a responsible, efficient and independent nonprofit organization funded solely by contributions from the American people. We are not a government agency nor do we receive any direct government funding.

National Statistics

- An industry-leading 93 cents of every dollar raised goes directly to programs and services.
- *Money* magazine named the American Red Cross one of the nation's 10 best-managed charities.
- The American Institute of Philanthropy has given the Red Cross an A+ rating for financial performance.
- In all, nearly 1.2 million trained Red Cross volunteers help people in their communities prevent, prepare for and cope with emergencies.

Mid-America Chapter Statistics

- Mid-America is the second-largest Chapter of the Red Cross in the nation, serving more than 8 million people.
- Locally, the Red Cross has 7,000 volunteers and 159 professional staff—a ratio of 44 to 1.
- The Chapter functions with an operating budget of $14.8 million, half coming from the United Way.
- 12 service centers in the metropolitan area.
- Territory: 4,110 square miles of northeastern Illinois, including Cook, DuPage, Kane, Kendall, Lake, McHenry and Will counties.

Our Values

Collaboration. We are committed to seizing and creating opportunities to achieve effective partnerships in the complex, diverse community we serve.

Community Focus. We concentrate our efforts on serving the specific needs of the complex and diverse urban, suburban and rural communities served.

Customer Satisfaction. We are dedicated to serving customers with only the highest quality products and services.

Diversity. We value diversity as a strength in our society. It is an integral part of providing quality programs and services to all communities.

Fiscal Independence. We seek to be fiscally independent of any one source or avenue of revenue.

Leadership. We encourage and support services, products and programs developed by the national organization and coordinate activities for ARC units throughout Illinois and across the country.

Quality Improvement. Our priorities are to increase the satisfaction of customers, clients and donors; decrease the time it takes to complete tasks; decrease expenditures; and increase funding.

Teamwork. We value and encourage our staff to work in groups by sharing resources, skills, knowledge and commitment in serving our customers.

Training and Development. We consistently attract, develop and utilize committed, professional colleagues who provide the highest quality of customer service and ensure effective and efficient delivery.

Volunteerism. We are a community-based volunteer organization governed, supported and principally staffed by volunteers who work with paid staff in all programs and services.

Our Strategic Positioning

The Leader. The American Red Cross in the Chicago metropolitan area seeks to expand its role and capacity as the region's leading nongovernmental disaster resource, responding immediately to its constituents' concerns.

The System. In allowing the customer to define "disaster," we need to define how we respond to the client—either directly or indirectly, by referring the client to an appropriate local agency. Referrals of clients to appropriate service providers will require the development of a highly automated, metro-wide information and referral system.

The services. While we will define how we respond to the customer's definition of "disaster," we currently have a functional department called Disaster Services. This department coordinates disaster community education; recurrent disaster response; nonrecurrent disaster preparedness and response; and the statewide staff center for nationally-administered disasters.

The Source. Once our information and referral disaster response network is operational and functioning effectively, the Mid-America Chapter will become the social service "information utility" for the metropolitan area, installing an outcomes measurement and management system to augment the information and referral network.

Joining Us in Knowing Us

The Red Cross in Chicago helps hundreds of thousands of people each year get beyond disasters and get on with their lives. To join us is to fully understand the services and programs we offer.

Our Disaster Services

We respond. Anytime a disaster strikes, the Red Cross responds at a moment's notice to help the victims rebuild their lives. Immediately following a disaster, we make sure disaster victims have food, clothing and a place to stay.

We assist. Once the emergency phase of a disaster has passed, trained Red Cross caseworkers meet with disaster victims and provide them with the means to get back on their feet. This is done by offering vouchers to purchase essentials such as food, new clothing, occupational tools, medicine, eyeglasses and furniture.

We comfort. As seen at work in Oklahoma City with the victims and families of individuals killed in the recent bombing, mental health workers are available to help people cope with the emotional aftermath of disasters. They provide a hand to hold, an ear to listen and a shoulder to rest on.

We study. All Red Cross disaster workers are trained by other Red Cross workers in all disaster-response disciplines (mass care, damage assessment, family service). This allows the entire organization to respond as efficiently as possible.

We donate. Disaster Services are offered to victims free of charge through the generous support of contributors. No repayment for disaster relief services is ever requested or expected. The Red Cross offers it as a gift from the American People.

Disaster statistics

- Last year, we responded to more than 2,000 disasters in the seven-county metropolitan area.
- We assisted more than 10,000 victims of disaster.
- We trained more than 200 to become volunteer disaster workers.
- We utilized more than $700,000 in public contributions to provide direct assistance to disaster victims.
- We coordinated Red Cross response to major flooding operations in 20 counties in central and southern Illinois.

Corporate & Community Education

We teach. The Red Cross offers safety and health education programs to corporations and community members to teach people how to avoid emergencies and change the outcomes of potentially fatal situations.

We coach. More lifeguards are trained by the Red Cross than all other organizations combined, making us the industry leader in aquatics safety programs.

We aid. First Aid/CPR courses show students how to "check, call and care" when an accident is encountered. One day in a Red Cross classroom can truly add to a lifetime.

We empower. AIDS is a killer and the Red Cross knows how to decrease the spread—education. Offering communities HIV educational courses aimed at culturally-diverse communities, the Red Cross has become a national training source for the latest information on the deadly epidemic.

Health Statistics

- Last year, we taught more than 123,000 young people how to be safe in the water and taught 8,400 swimmers the skills to be lifeguards.
- We aided more than 78,00 students in First-Aid/CPR courses.
- We empowered more than 44,000 to fight HIV/AIDS with up-to-date information.
- Overall, more than 260,000 individuals now have

the power to save a life—their own and someone else's life.

Social Services

We communicate. The Red Cross helps military members keep in touch with their families during personal family crises by providing verification of information for military leave and arranging for travel.

We link. Through International Tracing Services, the Red Cross helps local residents recover lost communications with relatives cut off from the rest of the world due to a natural disaster or civil unrest. Whether it was Bosnia or Kobe or Oklahoma City, the Red Cross has been and will continue to be a messenger of hope for people around the world.

We reunite. Holocaust Tracing Services aims to reunite surviving Holocaust victims with other family members who have survived the World War II persecution.

Social Service Statistics

- Last year more than 25,000 messages were communicated by the Mid-America Chapter.
- We linked dozens of families with relatives both in the United States and abroad, separated by civil unrest or natural disaster.

Our Research (Yankelovich)

We are loved. The American Red Cross is the most beloved of the American charities.

We are supportive. The Red Cross' commitment to support for the military and national disaster relief are valued contributions to American life.

We are dynamic. The Red Cross' strongest position is with young givers—those less than 35 years old—who see the Red Cross as active, dynamic and capable.

We have great potential. The Red Cross has a potential donor pool of as many as 60 percent of the 40 million American households that currently give more than $50 a year to a traditional charity. In addition, the Red Cross has an immediate opportunity with as many as 9 million American households.

We are valuable. The Red Cross' association with a corporate sponsor is very valuable. Research revealed that 60 percent of the American public would be more inclined to purchase a product associated with the Red Cross; the percentage is even higher—67 percent—for those between the ages of 21 and 34.

We are an option. If asked, a large portion of the public would give to the American Red Cross. This prompted the Red Cross to launch the 1995 Community Campaign as the largest ever for the organization. It provided the theme Help Can't Wait as a national creed; helping people caught in all types of emergencies.

OUR CURRENT NEEDS

The Mid-America Chapter is seeking potential candidates for two key positions for the Board of Directors:
- Vice Chair, Financial Development
- Vice Chair, Marketing

Objectives and Responsibilities Financial Development

There is a need to significantly expand the capacity of the Mid-America Chapter, to raise increasing amounts of operational support and to fund service and property strategies identified by our Board.

Candidates will:

- Have the ability to relate effectively with persons of wealth and influence regarding their personal, corporate and institutional financial support of the Mid-America Chapter and the American National Red Cross.

- Lead the Chapter's Annual Financial Development Campaign for three fiscal years beginning July 1, 1995 and ending June 30, 1998. The total campaign is $11 million during FY96 and increases a minimum of 7% per year.

- Work closely and effectively with staff to ensure the timely preparation of a comprehensive annual plan for Direct Response, Major Gifts, Corporate Foundations, Annual Gala (and other special events); Disaster Appeals; and Planned Giving programs.

- Provide leadership to the board and personally participate in the identification, screening and solicitation of individuals and organizations capable of making major gifts.

- Commit to a three-year term of an average of

five or more hours per week, adding personal and financial support to the Chapter appeals and functions.

- Have prior board experience in a major institution raising at least $3 to 5 million for annual operations and/or chaired a capital endowment campaign of $10 million over a five-year period.

Objectives and Responsibilities Marketing

The Mid-America Chapter will be positioned as the premier social service organization in Chicago, shifting focus from a product orientation to a customer orientation.

Candidates will:

- Possess leadership abilities to identify issues, develop organization-wide strategies and take action to implement effective marketing programs.

- Work closely with the Director of Marketing in the development of an integrated alignment of Marketing/Sales; Advertising/Public Relations; Direct Response; Marketing Research; Customer Service/Satisfaction; and Cause-Related Marketing.

- Lead in the continued development, expansion and modification of the marketing position of the American Red Cross as established in fiscal year 1995 during the first year of the annual campaign.

- Work closely and effectively with the staff in the development of an integrated marketing plan that reflects the strategies, objectives, tasks, responsibilities and timing for marketing activities throughout the Chapter.

- Advise in the creative, production, placement, distribution, evaluation and development of promotional activities, public service advertising and potential sponsored advertising.

- Oversee and advise in the development of a cross-unit team plan to develop and enhance the relationships between the Chapter and selected corporations with whom we seek to establish a strategic alliance.

- Provide professional direction and assistance in evaluating business development opportunities.

- Commit to a two-year term of an average of three or more hours per week, adding personal and financial support to the Chapter appeals and functions.

- Have 10 or more years of highly developed leadership experience in marketing, advertising and sales.

- Have the position of Senior Manager with a for-profit entity (revenues exceeding $1 billion).

Incentives for Board Members

Honor and prestige accompany the offer to join the Board of Directors of the American Red Cross. This offer is a one-of-a-kind opportunity to be an integral part of the leading source in human service, giving back to communities when they are in need of help.

Board members are a part of:

- the organization that translates your caring and concern into immediate action
- the premiere national social service agency
- an eager team of trained professionals that teach others how to deal with emergencies and save lives
- the disaster-relief agency often the first to arrive and the last to leave sites of local and national disasters
- one of the largest volunteer-based organizations in the United States with more than 1.2 million trained volunteers
- the charity held in the highest regard by top Chicago corporations, foundations and business leaders
- an international family of Red Cross/Red Crescent Societies with a worldwide presence in over 181 countries from Allentown to Zagreb (Croatia)
- the leading trend-setting health and safety education organization
- the organization providing needed services for military personnel and their families in Chicago and around the world

By contributing their time and energy to the Mid-America Chapter of the American Red Cross, the Board of Directors helps to make communities in and around Chicago—and around the world—a better, safer place to live.

This sample was provided by the Mid-America Chapter of the American Red Cross, Chicago, IL

CHAPTER

Research Board Candidate Sources

Recruit from multiple sources **79**

Why recruit from all levels? 79

Level #1: Friends and colleagues 80

Level #2: Members and patrons of your nonprofit 80

Level #3: Donors and contributors 80

Level #4: Researched sources 81

Accessing researched sources **81**

Where to start when you don't know what to do first 82

Phone tips for contacting potential candidate sources 83

Third-party referrals make candidate research easier 83

Leverage contacts for best referrals... 84

How many contacts are needed? 84

Fund development professional researches candidates........................ 84

Secure the fund development professional's help 85

When there's no fund development professional to call upon 85

Past prospects provide additional candidate sources 86

Keep records of contacts **86**

Computers simplify record keeping...................................... 87

STOP! Procedure checkpoint 87

Potential Board Candidate Sources 89

Targeted Board Recruitment Call Lists 90

CHAPTER

Research Board Candidate Sources

One of the problematic aspects of recruitment under the traditional nominating committee system is the tendency for committee members to recruit from a limited pool of board prospects. ■ Instead of pursuing high-profile candidates with demonstrated skills and clout in the community, many nominating committees approach their friends and colleagues. Those individuals, though often accomplished, don't necessarily have the right mix of skills that the board needs. As a result, these boards never reach their full potential. ■ I call this the Gerbil Syndrome—named after those little rodents that spend almost all their energy running on exercise wheels. ■ Boards that continually go back to their circles of friends to recruit new members are essentially imitating gerbils on a treadmill. They're content to do the same thing over and over again—even though it may not be to the greatest benefit of the organization. ■ This chapter is about breaking out of the Gerbil Syndrome. It explains how the development team can recruit better board members by moving beyond the traditional circle of friends. And it shows you where to find these individuals. ■

❏ RECRUIT FROM MULTIPLE SOURCES

Sources of potential board member candidates can be divided into four levels:

Level 1) Friends, colleagues and associates of current board members

Level 2) Members and patrons of your nonprofit

Level 3) Donors and contributors

Level 4) Researched sources, such as membership lists of professional organizations and alumni groups.

Think of these levels in the shape of an inverted pyramid (see graphic on Page 89). Level 4 is at the top, and Level 1—the circle of friends—is at the bottom.

The categories are arranged this way to represent the total number of potential board candidates and their relative importance in finding the ideal candidate. Level 1, friends, colleagues and associates of current board members, is at the bottom because it generates the fewest number of prospects that match specific requirements.

The board development team's goal should be to recruit from all levels. It should, however, concentrate on developing the majority of candidates from Level 4, researched sources.

Why recruit from all levels?

It's easy to understand why board members prefer to recruit from the circle of friends. Friends are accessible, easy to approach, and members probably won't have to talk to many of them before finding someone willing to make the commitment.

Boards, however, limit themselves by staying within this Level 1 category. By recruiting from all levels, development teams are likely to find that...

■ **The candidate pool is larger.** Let's assume you're looking for a candidate with public relations savvy. How many people do you personally know who are in public relations? Now compare that number with your answer to this question: How many people in your city, county or area work in the public relations field?

Obviously, you can't know everyone. The best candidate for the job may be someone who works in an office you're unfamiliar with. You won't know this, though, if you solicit only friends to join the board.

■ **Other sources provide qualified referrals.** If your friends aren't interested in the board position, who can they recommend? Usually, they suggest you call their own friends or acquaintances.

There's no guarantee that a friend of a friend will be any more qualified for a position than the acquaintance you originally asked. If you contacted a professional association—a Level 4 source—for referrals, you'd be more likely to receive the names of a number of highly qualified candidates.

■ **The likelihood of finding the right person is greater.** When recruiting board members, it's important to find a person who has the exact skills your board needs. The more candidates you talk to, the more likely it is that you'll find this person.

Again, though, it's impossible to know everyone. You must move beyond the circle of friends and interview board prospects from other sources.

Level #1: Friends and colleagues

These are people you interact with regularly, whether through work, social organizations or family. Although they may have some qualifications that you need on your board, they just as often have real limitations too.

The reason for this is simple: Your circle of friends, colleagues and associates is limited. You've read, for example, how one person can't know everyone in the community who belongs to a certain profession. But even when three or four of your friends fit the bill, you still hurt your organization by recruiting only them to the board.

Even though a friend or acquaintance has strong skills, he or she still may not measure up to the profile of an ideal candidate. There may be someone else in the community who is just as interested in your nonprofit and who is more skilled than your friend.

Level #2: Members and patrons of your nonprofit

Although the people who use your nonprofit's services may not be the best board prospects, they often know first-rate prospects. That's why it pays to stay in touch with high-profile members and patrons.

Members and patrons can also affect the recruiting process by suggesting ways to improve the organization.

For example, they might propose an additional program to meet the community's needs. If these same members or patrons also know someone experienced with that type of program, they can suggest that you contact him or her for help. This contact could be a potential board candidate.

Level #3: Donors and contributors

Donors and contributors are a frequently overlooked source for board member candidates and referrals. Several reasons make these individuals attractive contacts…

■ **Donors and contributors have a financial stake in the organization.** Individuals who contribute to your nonprofit want their contributions to make a difference. They also want to know that the nonprofit is being effectively managed. If approached with a board membership opportunity, many donors will show interest in the recruiting process.

■ **Donors provide high-quality referrals.** This is true for two reasons: First, donors tend to recommend people of the same community status that they are. If you contact a high-profile donor, you'll likely get a high-profile referral.

Second, many donors—especially major donors—have personal contacts in the investment and/or money management profession. If asked for a referral in this skill area, donors are likely to recommend qualified prospects whom they've had success with personally.

■ **Contact with donors and contributors is easy.** For one thing, it's already being done by the fund development department. Donors and contributors are regularly informed of nonprofit events and called on for making gifts. A few words about board service could easily be added to these calls, making additional phone work unnecessary.

■ **Individuals who donate money or in-kind gifts to your nonprofit believe in its mission.** They know the organization makes a difference in people's lives. If donors didn't believe this, they wouldn't give. That is why it's far easier to sell donors on the benefits of board service.

To take advantage of this candidate resource, talk with your nonprofit's fund development professional. He or she regularly updates the organization's list of donors and contributors. Ask him or her to provide it for the board development team.

Level #4: Researched sources

Researched sources include individuals who are outside of the categories that include friends, acquaintances, members, patrons or donors. Researched sources are members of professional associations, clubs, Chambers of Commerce and alumni groups.

In fact, a researched source can be just about anything. Here's a partial list of some common sources:

Alumni organizations
Associations
Athletic organizations
Business and trade associations
Chambers of Commerce
Clubs
Fraternal organizations
Human service organizations
Professional organizations (e.g., National Society of Fund Raising Executives, Association of Certified Public Accountants)
Publications
Religious organizations
Senior citizen services and organizations
Veterans and military organizations
Women's organizations and services
Youth organizations

Hundreds of thousands of people belong to these types of organizations. That makes this the largest—and potentially the most productive—source of board prospects. This is why professional recruiters often begin here when searching for potential job candidates.

Researched sources, however, can be intimidating. They're often perceived as large, impersonal groups that only help their members—not nonprofit board members trying to improve their organization.

That simply isn't true. Researched sources are easy to access if you take a deliberate and organized approach.

❏ ACCESSING RESEARCHED SOURCES

Granted, some researched sources, like alumni associations, put limits on who can obtain their membership lists—so you'll have to use your connections to get what you need.

Other sources, though, are easy to tap into.

The first step in accessing a researched source is to make a list of all researched sources where you believe potential board candidates may be found.

So if you're looking for a marketing professional, the first researched source on your list should be the local chapter of the American Marketing Association, a national professional organization. Obviously, professional organizations are the best place to find large numbers of people with specific professional expertise.

The next entry on your list should be the local Chamber of Commerce. Representatives there can tell you where most of the local marketing professionals are and, perhaps, pass along a name or two.

You should also include on the list the names of any area marketing firms. They're also potential board member sources.

After you have a comprehensive list compiled, start calling. The person to talk to at associations, clubs and the Chamber of Commerce is the executive director. He or she will be able to give you the information you need. When calling commercial firms, talk first with the marketing director (even when you're not looking for a marketing-oriented candidate). This person can tell you if the firm gives referrals and, if so, whom to talk to about them.

Gaining access to non-public researched sources, like alumni organizations and club membership lists, is a little trickier. Often, these organizations only release information about members to other members. For example, if you're trying to obtain a college alumni list, you'll discover that those lists typically are available only to graduates of the school.

To gain access to these organizations, you must contact individuals who belong to that organization who can help you. For example,

if you're trying to get an alumni list from the local university, ask other board members, friends, patrons and donors if they are graduates of the school or if they know someone who is.

Then contact the alum and explain your nonprofit's goals, what you're looking for in a board member and what you need him or her to do. Most of the time this individual will gladly contact the university alumni office, request a list and send you a copy of it.

Where to start when you don't know what to do first

If you're looking for a specific kind of board candidate, but don't have the slightest idea where that person might be found, you can get help from these two sources:

■ **The library.** When you're at a loss over where to find someone, go to the library. Research librarians are excellent at identifying and locating groups of people. They can also show you how to use various directories and the reference section of the library—so you can locate key people on your own in the future.

■ **The Yellow Pages.** If you're wondering whether your community has a specific professional organization, just open the phone book. Look in the Yellow Pages under "Associations" for a list.

Remember, though, that the Yellow Pages is not always a complete listing. There may be additional associations in the community that choose not to pay for a Yellow Pages entry. For a comprehensive list of associations, consult your research librarian.

Phone tips for contacting potential candidate sources

Calling candidate sources on the phone can be a little nerve-racking at first. But it gets easier—especially if you apply this tip: Always tell the phone contact that you need his or her help.

Most people who belong to organizations, especially professional organizations, are successful, established people who are looking for ways to give something back to the community. If you tell them up front that you—and your nonprofit—need their help, nine out of 10 will do what they can to help you reach your goal.

Here's a practice exercise that you can use to get your feet wet:

Look in the Yellow Pages to find the professional organization you're targeting. With a position profile in hand, call and introduce yourself. For example, you can say:

"Hello, my name is John Doe. I'm the executive director at XYZ Nonprofit. I'm calling today because I need your help.

"We're in the early stages of an important board development campaign, and what I would like to do is spend a few minutes giving you an overview of the ideal candidate profile. We're looking for someone who matches this profile. Is now a convenient time or should I call back later?"

If convenient, give the contact a two- or three-minute recap of the scripted story and the position profile. Then ask this question: "Who within your organization should I be talking to about this important position?"

Usually this contact person, who doesn't know you at all, will provide two, three or four names of possible prospects. Now you're

in a position to contact those people. However, this second call will be easier because you now have a third-party referral.

Third-party referrals make candidate research easier

Here's a universal truth: It's always easier to get someone's attention or cooperation when you can say you were referred by a person he or she knows.

Take the phone call to a researched source that was just described. It was a cold call. You didn't know the person who you were calling, and he or she didn't know who you were or what you wanted.

A third-party referral makes this kind of call easier. Because the prospect knows and trusts the party who referred you, he or she is more likely to listen to you.

For example, you've just called an association and receive some referrals from its executive director. When you contact them, use the name of the executive director when introducing yourself. The referrals won't know you, but they will know the executive director.

This takes some of the edge off the call for both you and the individuals you're calling. For referrals, it gives the call credibility. People won't usually refer callers to their friends, colleagues and acquaintances if they don't believe a project is legitimate.

So if a prospect knows that you were referred to him or her by one of these people, you're more likely to be perceived as someone who deserves the prospect's attention.

The third-party referral also works because it will be easier to capture prospects' attention and explain your situation. Without a referral, prospects may not talk with you at all or quickly dismiss the contact as an unwanted solicitation call.

Leverage contacts for best referrals

Sometimes, those you call just won't be the right people. They either won't be interested, or they won't match the criteria in your position profile.

When this happens, ask them for referrals who do match the profile criteria. In other words, leverage your contacts.

Leveraging can open all kinds of doors for the board development team. Assume that you're after a specific company president, for example, but don't know anyone who can give you the "in" you need. You can reach this targeted prospect by networking with individuals who can eventually introduce you.

Networking, in this instance, is synonymous with leveraging. It's a process of strategically contacting individuals that will lead you to the potential candidate, or who will give you third-party referrals to individuals who are one step closer to the target.

Your role as the caller is to describe the type of person you're looking for in a way that will lead the listener to refer you to the targeted prospect. Ideally, you will end up talking with the company president you wanted in the first place—and be able to use a third-party referral to introduce yourself.

How many contacts are needed?

When researching contacts, it's important to remember that not everyone who is contacted about serving on a board will accept. Some contacts will turn you down right away. Others will drop out during the selection process, and a few just won't fit the profile.

This means that the initial list of possible board member contacts should be as long as possible.

A general rule is that about half the original prospects will talk with you to learn more about your nonprofit. Of that half, about a third will make it all the way to the final selection.

Here's how that looks in actual numbers:

If you contact 20 prospects, only 10 will probably be interested or qualified enough to meet with you personally. Of those 10, seven (two-thirds of 10) will probably drop out somewhere in the process. This leaves you with three serious candidates for one board position.

Ideally, you should generate from 15 to 20 contacts for each board position. (Fewer will be needed as the development team improves its screening techniques.) This guarantees that you will have a choice of finalists when the time comes to select new board members. Because you have a choice, you can choose the best person for the job—instead of being "stuck" with whoever happens to have made it through the entire selection process.

Fund development professional researches candidates

The member of the board development team best suited to do board prospect research is your nonprofit's fund development professional.

He or she will require very little training to

complete this assignment. As the Number One fund raiser at your organization, this individual is experienced and comfortable calling people, and introducing himself or herself and the nonprofit. Plus, the fund development department already has a long list of donor names and telephone numbers to start working from.

Having the fund development professional do the research also makes it easier to persuade other development team members to make formal recruiting contacts. If given a list of people to contact, their telephone numbers, a third-party referral to use and a summary of how they may be able to help the nonprofit, development team members are much more enthusiastic about making calls.

Secure the fund development professional's help

Because the fund development director is part of the board development team, he or she is usually willing to take on this project. In some cases, though, the fund development professional may balk at doing this research in addition to his or her regular duties.

If that happens, here's how to persuade the fund development professional to take on this responsibility:

■ **Explain how his or her research will actually make the fund development job easier.** For example, emphasize how research can ultimately improve the commitment and giving ability of the board.

If the fund development professional is researching board contacts, he or she can look for prospects who can give and get significant funds. That, in turn, makes the board more effective at fund raising—which makes the fund development professional's job easier.

■ **Offer to hire someone who can help.** If your nonprofit's development department is always busy, you might have to make some concessions. For example, you may need to hire a part-time staff member to help with the research or to complete other department tasks while the fund development director researches board candidate prospects.

Graduate students in business or research fields are excellent sources of help with this. They're detail-oriented and skilled at finding information—both of which are very important to successful prospect research.

When there's no fund development professional to call upon

Obviously, organizations too small to have a regular fund development professional won't be able to take advantage of that expertise and experience during the contact research phase of the recruitment process.

If this affects you, you'll have to rely on the experience of the board development team to compile a list of prospective contacts. One team member should coordinate this effort.

The individual chosen may have to recruit other people to help him or her make initial research contacts. Like a fund development professional, he or she should seek out the help of detail-oriented people and work closely with a research librarian to identify groups of board prospects. The research leader must also make regular reports to the development team captain, just as the fund development professional would.

Past prospects provide additional candidate sources

Each time you use the strategic board recruitment process, it becomes easier to identify qualified prospects. This can be attributed to two factors.

First, the development team is becoming more efficient in using the process, and more confident in tapping the resources available to it.

A second reason for the improvement is the development team's past networking. Each time team members meet with prospective candidates, they acquaint themselves with a high-profile contact and introduce a prospect to their organization. The team may even invite the prospect to get involved with the organization as a board committee member.

Over time, the number of people whom the development team meets and invites to work on committee-related projects grows. As a result, team members have a fifth source of potential board candidates—past prospects who for some reason did not or could not serve on the board when first approached.

Editor's Note: More about inviting prospects to work on board committees is in Chapter 8.

❏ KEEP RECORDS OF CONTACTS

It's very important to keep organized records of the work you do during the candidate research process.

In fact, record keeping related to specific board candidates should begin the first time the development team talks about potential board member sources. This usually is at the first board meeting when the position profiles are unveiled.

After discussing the profiles, the full board should help development team members add to its initial list of possible sources. These additional sources may include specific individuals, or they may be organizations, clubs or associations.

These names will then be placed on a Targeted Board Recruitment Call List (see Page 90), and turned over to the fund development professional.

This form includes space for the name of the individual, his or her organization, professional position and telephone number. Each entry also has space for the name of a third party who suggested that you contact the individual. At the top of the sheet is space to track where contacts come from. For instance, is a contact best described as part of the corporate sector or part of the government? After deciding, team members can put a hash mark beside the appropriate category.

Using these Call Lists, the fund development professional will begin making contacts and gathering information and referrals from these individuals and/or organizations.

After the fund development professional has gathered the names, the information from each contact is transferred to a Board Recruiting Contact Sheet. The Contact Sheets are then distributed to the board development team members and used to record the outcome of all formal contacts. (More about this process is in Chapter 7. A copy of the sheet is on Page 118.)

Computers simplify record keeping

Board development team members must complete a new Contact Sheet each time they speak with a candidate. This information is then stored in a central location, so the records of all contacts with a particular individual can be found quickly.

This record-keeping process can be made easier by using a computer and a database software program. After a contact, the information from the call list can be entered into the appropriate fields. To see the running history the development team has established with an individual, team members can either read from the computer screen or—in two or three keystrokes—print out a hard copy.

A system similar to this may already be up and running in your nonprofit's fund development office. If possible, share it.

Simply add the relevant entry fields for recruitment information to the existing donor list. This way, you save the time you would have spent setting up your own system, and you can take advantage of a reliable data entry system that's already been established. ■

STOP! Procedure checkpoint

Before moving on to Step 6 of the strategic recruiting process, Develop Third-Party Referral Networks, have you...

❑ Discussed with development team members the importance of recruiting from all source levels?

❑ Outlined the different source levels and how they can be accessed?

❑ Talked with the fund development professional about using the current donor list to research prospective board members?

❑ Made a list of groups where you believe candidates that fit your position profiles will be found?

- Continued -

❏   Contacted the research librarian for help in identifying additional candidate sources?

❏   Approached the fund development professional about performing initial candidate research?

❏   Recorded all possible sources on a Board Recruitment Call List?

❏   Created a computer database file to store all recruitment information?

Fund development professional, have you...

❏   Practiced making a telephone research contact? (Do this with another team development member.)

❏   Collected as many third-party referrals as possible?

❏   Recorded the outcome of all telephone contacts on a Board Recruiting Contact Sheet?

POTENTIAL BOARD CANDIDATE SOURCES

SOURCE LEVELS

4   **Researched sources**

3   **Donors and contributors**

2   **Members and patrons**

1   **Friends, colleagues and associates**

The higher the source level, the larger the pool of qualified board candidates. All board development teams should strive to recruit primarily from Source Level 4, Researched sources. Among these sources are alumni organizations, associations, Chambers of Commerce, professional organizations and clubs.

TARGETED BOARD RECRUITMENT CALL LISTS

Patrons/constituents _____   Donor _____

Social _____   Professional _____

Corporate _____   Government _____

Foundations _____   Other _____

Name	Organization	Position	Phone
1.			
Third-party referral source:			
2.			
Third-party referral source:			
3.			
Third-party referral source:			
4.			
Third-party referral source:			
5.			
Third-party referral source:			
6.			
Third-party referral source:			
7.			
Third-party referral source:			
8.			
Third-party referral source:			

CHAPTER

Develop Third-Party Referral Networks

Referral networks defined **95**
How nonprofits use referral networks 95
Developing a referral network 96
Target the best companies and organizations for a network 96
Institutionalize network relationships **97**
Create relationships slowly 97
Build a referral network without adding board members 98
Beneficial affiliations for all networks 98
Referral networks outlive traditional nominating committee networks 98
Second-generation development teams expand network 99
STOP! Procedure checkpoint 100
    Structure of a Network 101
    Evolution of a Network 102

CHAPTER

Develop Third-Party Referral Networks

When an organization begins using the strategic recruiting process, the bulk of work is completed by board development team members. They find out where prospective candidates are, research their backgrounds and build relationships with them. ■ Eventually, though, you'll want to take the recruiting process to a point where it's not so labor-intensive. One effective way to do this is to develop third-party referral networks. ■ These networks are individuals, and business and specialty groups within the community—like banking, education and government—that have an ongoing relationship with your organization. They provide information, resources and expertise that helps the nonprofit achieve its goals, in addition to providing access to potential board members and volunteers. ■ This chapter explains how third-party referral networks are established and used. It also tells you why they're invaluable to your board. ■

❏ REFERRAL NETWORKS DEFINED

To understand third-party referral networks, it's important to first distinguish the third-party referral network from a simple third-party referral.

A third-party referral is related to people. It's a recommendation from one person to contact another person for help.

If your family doctor tells you to see a specialist about a medical problem, that's a referral. It's also a referral when you contact businessperson Jane Doe for assistance, and she recommends that you call businessperson John Jones.

Third-party referrals make it quick and easy to get your foot in the door of an organization. This is because the third party is a ready-made connection with the person or group you're trying to start a relationship with.

The third-party referral network, however, is much more complex. A network focuses on groups, rather than on individual persons, and is used for the benefit of the whole nonprofit.

A referral network is a group of organizations that is permanently associated with your nonprofit. Because of this association, the nonprofit has access to information and expertise of each group that will help the nonprofit reach its goals. These network organizations may also provide board prospect referrals.

For example, your nonprofit might work frequently with a specific bank, local government or a university. Or the nonprofit might have employees from each institution on its board. This connection gives you an "in" with these groups. When your nonprofit needs to solve a problem related to one of these groups' business, you have a contact to call upon.

A graphic representation of a first-generation referral network is on Page 101.

How nonprofits use referral networks

A third-party referral network is a constant resource that your nonprofit can call on for help. This help usually takes two forms:

■ **Information that affects nonprofit plans.** When your nonprofit is connected with another organization, it has access to the expertise and information that organization provides. Your board can use this information to reach goals and prepare the nonprofit for the future.

For example, if your organization deals with abused children, you should associate yourself with the state and city government. These groups often regulate how shelters operate, provide funding and refer children for services.

Because these agencies affect how your nonprofit operates from day to day, it pays to have friends in those circles. Those individuals can help you stay a step ahead of other service providers by explaining how new laws affect you, making recommendations on how to comply with them and providing information or statistics to help you develop new programs.

■ **Future board member sources.** Third-party referral networks are also excellent sources for board candidates. If you've established relationships with various professional organizations, for instance, it will be much easier for development team members to reach someone who can recommend up-and-coming professionals for board positions.

The initial telephone contact with the association is easier to make because team members don't have to explain everything about the organization and why it needs the association's help. And because the association is already familiar with your nonprofit, it can provide even better, more-qualified referrals.

Developing a referral network

The board development team will create a third-party referral network in much the same way it recruits individual board members.

It should begin by reviewing the organization's needs and goals. Then the team must look for groups within the community that can help the nonprofit meet its needs and reach its goals.

When appropriate groups have been identified, team members should start recruiting board members from them. This establishes an initial connection with the organization that your nonprofit needs assistance from.

To understand how this process works, let's assume that your nonprofit wants to develop a planned giving program to increase its endowment.

An excellent place to turn for help is the financial services and insurance sectors of the business community. Financial planners and life insurance professionals are a source of knowledgeable people on the subject of planned giving options. They're also experi-

enced in educating their clients about planned giving. It's only logical that development team members should target these individuals as potential board prospects.

After a financial planner or life insurance professional has joined your organization's board, the nonprofit has access to his or her professional expertise and resources. The board development team will also have a means to establish a third-party referral network with the new board member's firm.

Target the best companies and organizations for a network

When recruiting with the goal of developing a future third-party referral network, the board development team will focus as much on the type of organization that will benefit the nonprofit as the specific type of person.

Just as it does when identifying board member prospects, the development team should pursue only the best firms and organizations to become part of its third-party referral network. The reason is obvious: If you want to be the best, then you have to work with the best.

Examples of this are everywhere: Musicians who want to perform at the top of their field practice with the best teachers. Athletes who want to win championships train with the best coaches.

If your nonprofit wants to establish itself as the best service provider, the expertise it relies on must come from the best people. So if a bank is part of your third-party referral network, ideally it should be the leading bank in the area.

Action: When identifying prospective

board candidates, give as much attention to prospects' contacts and employers as to their personal and professional qualities. Instead of asking, "Who do we know that fits this pro-file?" single out the top firm in the area and ask, "Who do we know at this firm that fits this profile?" or "Who do we know at this firm that can provide a quality candidate referral?"

❏ INSTITUTIONALIZE NETWORK RELATIONSHIPS

When a new board member is installed, the only relationship that exists is between that individual and the board development team.

To build a strong third-party network, however, this relationship must be expanded and transferred. The connection must evolve from a person-to-person relationship—which it currently is—to a person-to-institution relationship to an institution-to-institution relationship.

Create relationships slowly

Building this alliance between your nonprofit and the board member's organization is a gradual process. Pushing for an immediate partnership will make the board member feel as if he or she was just the means to an end—which may sap his or her enthusiasm. The organization itself also may feel that you're making inappropriate demands of it.

To create an institution-to-institution relationship, start small and use the resources you already have access to. For example, involve the new board member in a major project. Then recognize the board member for his or her contribution and single out his or her firm or company as well.

Continue recognizing the board member's professional expertise and the quality firm he or she works for. When you know that the firm is pleased with the attention it's getting, start building the relationship in other ways.

Ask the board member to approach the CEO about participating in or sponsoring a fund raising event, or making a gift to the nonprofit. Then publicly thank the company for its help.

This generates a lot of positive public relations for the firm, and it connects the company directly to the nonprofit's mission. It also begins to involve people from the firm other than the board member—e.g., the company's CEO and possibly vice presidents or human resources representatives.

Once these people are involved, you can talk about the possibility of setting up an employee volunteer program—where corporate employees donate their time to help nonprofit staff members and the people the organization serves. Or you could discuss other types of partnerships.

By the time the board member completes his or her term, a relationship between the nonprofit and the firm is in place. It will continue regardless of who's on the board or who's on the board development team.

Build a referral network without adding board members

There are some groups that your organization will want as part of its referral network that won't be appropriate places to recruit board members from.

A good example of this is a professional organization. Although it can be an excellent source of referrals, the chances are that its staff members don't have the level of expertise and clout you need on your board. There's another reason for not recruiting these individuals: Your main interest in the organization they work for is the contacts it can provide.

Building a relationship with this type of organization will have to be done differently than with organizations that have staff members on your board.

This generally begins with basic networking. The development team will establish a relationship with an organization contact person as it continues asking for candidate referrals. Gradually, the development team could suggest collaborative projects between the nonprofit and the professional organization, like a special event fund raiser. That would serve as a means to introduce staff members at both organizations to one another and set the stage for an ongoing relationship.

Beneficial affiliations for all networks

Although your organization's third-party referral network should be built around your specific needs, nonprofits can benefit substantially from associating with the following groups:

- **Government.** Connections with government agencies can pay off with instant information about new laws or regulations, the status of legislation, tips on complying with current laws and regulations and, possibly, advice on how to lobby legislators.
- **Banking.** Without money, your nonprofit can't function—so it's only logical that you seek counsel from someone inside the financial world. Although this person won't manage organization funds personally, he or she can advise you on how to earn maximum returns on investments and build an endowment that can support the nonprofit in the future.
- **Specialty adviser.** If your nonprofit isn't affiliated with financial and estate planners, life insurance professionals, corporate and community leaders, educators, public and community relations specialists, medical, legal and accounting experts, and executive search professionals, it should be.
- **Marketing and community relations.** All organizations need a good public image to be successful. Contacts and board members from these circles can help you build awareness of your nonprofit in the community and increase use of its services.

Organizations should develop the remaining networks based on their mission and needs. Some examples of other networks include higher education, corporations, professional associations, fund development organizations and the media.

Referral networks outlive traditional nominating committee networks

The beauty of the third-party referral network system is that it outlives the board development team and the board. No matter who is serving in either group, the same referral networks are available.

This gives your board a huge advantage over boards that use nominating committees.

Because nominating committees tend to work from within their circle of friends, the networks available to the nonprofit are the personal networks of committee members. When a committee member leaves the board, so does his or her network of contacts.

The result of this is that the board and nominating committee must always establish a new network. There's no consistency from one nominating committee to the next, and no guarantee that the nonprofit will always have contacts in a certain field.

A third-party referral system, however, has been "institutionalized." A personal relationship has become an institutional relationship. The network belongs to the nonprofit—not individual board development team members.

Because of this, the network stays intact when development team members step down. Oncoming team members can continue to take advantage of the contacts.

Second-generation development teams expand network

Since the basic third-party referral network structure remains intact as board development team members change, the role of second- and third-generation teams is to expand the network.

For example, the second-generation development team may add more groups to the original structure. It may add banking and higher education to the group of organizations already part of the network.

Another way for team members to expand the network is for them to make additional contacts within a specific organization. For instance, team members may pursue additional contacts in the group "government," so that it can be divided into two groups: local government and state government.

To visualize how this evolution takes place, turn to the graphic, "Evolution of a Network," on Page 102. ■

STOP! Procedure checkpoint

Before moving on to Step 7 of the strategic recruiting process, Contact and Meet Candidate Prospects, have you...

❑ Discussed third-party referral networks with the development team?

❑ Identified groups in your community that may be of assistance to your organization?

❑ Identified anyone at those groups who may serve as a third-party referral into the groups?

❑ Contacted those groups to talk about your board development project and the position profiles you're trying to fill?

❑ Begun carefully building relationships with groups who already have representatives on your nonprofit's board?

STRUCTURE OF A NETWORK

First-Generation Referral Network

Board development teams should always be aware of groups within the community that can help their nonprofits attain goals. Gradually, the development team should build relationships with these groups so the nonprofit board can "reach out" to one of them for assistance when needed.

EVOLUTION OF A NETWORK

Second-Generation Referral Network

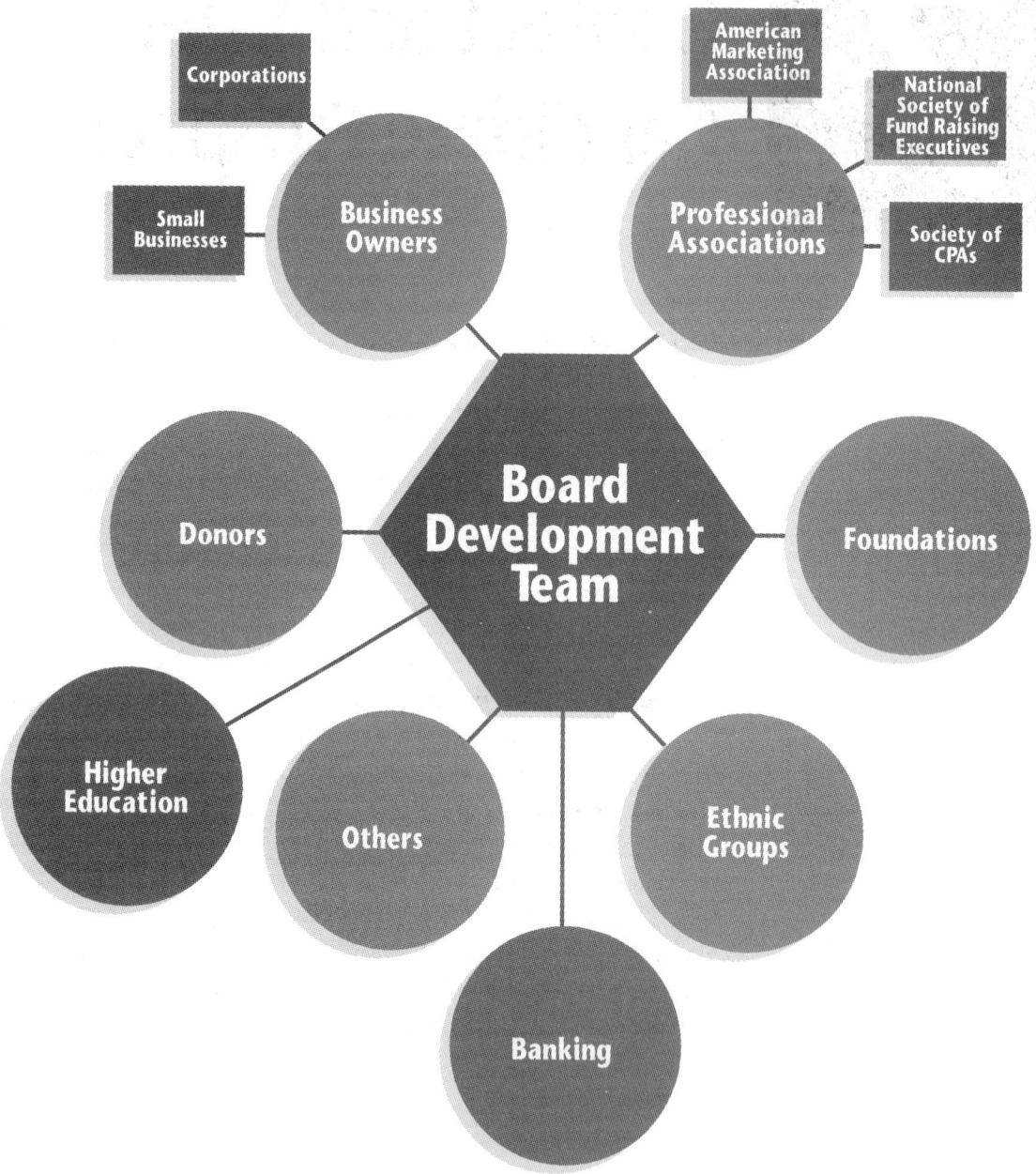

As the second- and third-generation board development teams are formed, the existing network remains. The task of succeeding development teams is to add new groups to the network (see higher education and banking), and to expand and diversify existing network groups (see professional organizations and business owners).

CHAPTER

Contact and Meet Candidate Prospects

Start the contact process **107**
Group meetings are most productive 107
How to meet highest-profile prospects 107
The first contact: An introductory telephone call 108
Tips for successful telephone contacts 108
Sample telephone conversation 110
Redirect the phone call when contacts seem uninterested 110
Move on after a negative contact 111
Use other recruitment tools to follow up telephone contacts 111
Practice makes interviews perfect 112
Conduct face-to-face meetings **112**
Let prospects share their feelings about the opportunity 113
When personal interviews go badly 114
Maintain records of all contacts **115**
Record information on Candidate Information Form 115
Development team reports 115
Continuous contacts give development team a choice....................... 116
STOP! Procedure checkpoint 117
    Board Recruiting Contacts 118
    Board Candidate Information 119

CHAPTER 7

Contact and Meet Candidate Prospects

One of the more intimidating aspects of recruiting new board members is approaching prospective candidates. Many individuals are afraid of saying the wrong things, not being able to answer candidates' questions and being flat out turned down. ■ This is why so many boards recruit only from their circles of friends. Friends are easy to approach and more likely to join a board than a stranger from the business community. ■ This chapter addresses how to get over the initial anxiety of recruiting, so you can feel comfortable approaching anyone about serving on the board. Included are tips on talking to candidates, from the first telephone call through the personal interview process. It also shows you how to use the other tools of strategic recruiting—position profiles and the scripted story—to make recruitment contacts even easier. ■

❏ START THE CONTACT PROCESS

The fund development professional or main fund raiser, as explained in Chapter 5, is responsible for compiling a list of prospective board candidates using referrals from other board members, nonprofit patrons, donors and researched sources.

At the end of this process, the fund development professional prepares the final list for the board development team. He or she does this by transferring all potential contacts' names from the Targeted Board Recruitment Call List to general Board Recruiting Contacts sheets. (Copies of these forms are on Pages 90 and 118.) These sheets are then divided among the development team members, and it becomes their responsibility for calling board prospects.

Development team members will make these contacts in two phases: Phase One is the initial telephone contact. It's an opportunity for the team member to introduce himself or herself and the nonprofit, and to briefly explain the board recruitment process. If the contact shows interest, the caller can arrange for Phase Two—a face-to-face meeting.

Group meetings are most productive

Personal meetings with contacts should be conducted in groups or teams. For example, if your board development team has six members, you may divide into three teams of two, or two teams of three. This helps team members several ways:

First, it reduces the stress that members feel when meeting prospects. A team member who meets with a prospect alone has little support going into the situation, and no one to fall back on if the meeting goes poorly. When team members work in groups, however, one can fall back on the other if something goes wrong. As a result, they can relax and give better presentations.

A second benefit of meeting in teams is that the presentation itself can be divided among team members. Individual members then will have less information to remember—which means the presentation will be better-prepared and presented. And the better-presented your story is, the easier it is to hold prospects' attention.

Also when working in teams, members can rehearse with each other and hear constructive criticism about how they present their segment. This, too, improves the presentation's overall quality.

How to meet highest-profile prospects

For the highest-profile board prospects, like well-established, successful businesspeople and community leaders, the contact process is slightly different. Instead of calling directly, send a formal letter introducing yourself.

Include the same basic information that you would convey during a phone call—who you are, what you're doing and what you want. The letter also should include the names of development team members and their credentials, as well as a date and time you plan to call the individual about this opportunity.

This type of written introduction conveys respect for the prospect and his or her accomplishments. It can also increase the likelihood of earning that person's cooperation. For example, if you explain that you'll be calling at a certain time, this high-profile prospect may reserve time to talk with you. If you don't send a letter, however—and just try calling—the chances are that you won't get any further than leaving your name and telephone number.

Personal meetings with high-profile prospects should also be handled differently than other meetings. Instead of sending any two members of the board development team, send the three team leaders—usually the executive director, the fund development professional and the board chairperson.

These people are important for two reasons: First, they're the most knowledgeable of the three plans and their goals. That means they'll be comfortable presenting this information and answering questions.

The second reason team leaders should make the call is the tendency for high-profile people to be impressed by other high-profile people. If the prospect knows that your organization has sent its three top leaders to make the presentation, it makes him or her feel important. It also communicates to the prospect that it's highly important that your organization get his or her cooperation.

The first contact:
An introductory telephone call

The first contact with board member prospects is usually by telephone. This should be short, about two or three minutes, and its primary goal should be to let prospects know who you are and what you're doing.

During these initial calls, it's important that development team members don't pressure prospects to join the board. At this point, you're just introducing yourself and trying to find out if they're interested in learning more about your nonprofit.

Before making a contact, however, it helps to review any information about that individual available to you; for example, a personal background or work history. This will help you get a sense of who the prospect is and what is important to him or her—and it may help you relax and more easily connect with the individual.

Information such as work histories, hobbies and other nonprofit-related activities is frequently gathered about nonprofit contributors. Check with your fund development professional to see if he or she has something on file about potential board member prospects.

Tips for successful telephone contacts

There are several ways for board development team members to maximize their success when making telephone calls to board prospects. These include...

■ **Be conscientious of the contact's schedule.** Prospective board member candidates are often busy people—especially if they hold high-profile jobs. That's why it's important to ask prospects up front, "Is now a good time to talk, or should I call back later?"

If you don't, you risk losing the prospect altogether. A development team member who calls a prospect and immediately launches into the nonprofit's scripted story, for example, may be interrupting a meeting or other important work time. This puts the prospect in the position of having to cut off the team member in mid-stride. As a result, the prospect may, out of frustration, say "no" immediately or be impatient when the team member calls back.

On the other hand, asking if you should call back later sends the message to prospects that you respect their work and their schedules. It also implies that you're willing to cooperate to reach a goal—rather than just making demands and expecting results. Therefore, it's more likely that they will schedule some time to focus on the opportunity you're presenting.

■ **Avoid making the conversation sound like a sales call.** Most people dislike telemarketing calls, so it's important to quickly distinguish your recruiting call from one.

The key to this is to stress what you're doing—whether it's general board development or something specific, like writing a new marketing plan. This piques listeners' interest because they'll wonder how they fit into your picture.

For example, you can say:

"Hello, my name is Jack Smith. I'm (executive director/a member of the board development team) for XYZ Nonprofit. We are in the initial stages of talking with (area of need) experts like yourself about a key position on our board of directors. You've been referred to us by (third-party referral name) as someone who has a strong background in (area of need).

"I was wondering whether I could talk with you a few minutes about this opportunity. Is now a good time or should I call back later?"

In this situation, you've put your cards on the table right away. The listener knows who you are and what you're doing, and very little time has passed. You're both now in a position to decide whether the opportunity is worth pursuing.

Don't, however, approach prospects in this manner:

"Hello, my name is Jack Smith. I'm (executive director/a member of the board development team) for XYZ Nonprofit. I'm not sure if you've heard of our organization. As a homeless shelter, we provide food and shelter for several hundred area residents each week. We also work closely with the city council on solutions to this problem."

By this point, most listeners will think you're about to solicit them for money or an in-kind donation.

They also will have already decided their answer to this particular question—and will tune out anything else you may say, like what it is that you're really doing.

Action: When introducing yourself, don't spend a lot of time talking about who you are or the organization you're calling for because listeners will anticipate some kind of solicitation. Instead, introduce yourself and describe the specific purpose of your call.

■ **Use a third-party referral right away.** If you've been referred to a board prospect by someone else, use that third party's name during your introduction.

For example, you might begin the conversation by saying, "My name is Jane Doe, and I'm with ABC Nonprofit. We're in the initial stages of talking with (area of need) experts like yourself about a key position on our board of directors. Joe Smith suggested that you could be someone who can help us. Is now a good time to talk or should I call back at a different time?"

Because you've immediately used the name of someone the prospect knows, the contact is effectively drawn into the conversation. Out of curiosity and respect for his or her acquaintance, the prospect will usually be more attentive and helpful.

Another effective contact strategy is to ask the third-party to call their referral on your behalf—then all the board development team has to do is follow up on the contact.

Sample telephone conversation

All board development team members will have their own personal style on the telephone. All phone contacts, however, should follow the same general pattern—and make their point quickly.

Here's how the first segment of a typical telephone contact might go…

Board development team member:

"Hello, my name is Jack Smith. I'm the (executive director/board development team member) at XYZ Nonprofit. Jane Doe suggested that you could be someone who could help us. Is now a good time to talk, or should I call back at a different time?"

Contact source:

"Yes, now is fine."

Team member:

"Well, we're in the initial stages of talking with experts like yourself regarding a key position on our nonprofit's board. If I may, I'll briefly describe for you our Ideal Candidate Profile. Who do you know that matches our profile, or might you personally be interested?"

At this point, the prospect will indicate his or her interest. If he or she would like to know more, the team member should arrange a personal meeting to talk at length about current board projects and the organization's long-range needs.

Redirect the phone call when contacts seem uninterested

Some prospects just won't be interested in what you're doing, or they'll simply be too busy to help. Don't be upset by these responses. They're a common part of the recruiting process.

A rejection, however, doesn't automatically mean that a prospect is a lost cause. Depending on the tone of the conversation, the team member may either redirect or abandon the call. Here's how…

■ **Redirecting the call.** This simply means changing the goal of your call. Instead of talking to the person as a potential board member candidate, for example, you can shift the talk to volunteer opportunities or making a donation. Or you can use the call as an opportunity to ask for referrals who fit the position profile.

Redirecting a call is simple. For instance, the person on the other end of the phone might say, "Well, I'm on three boards already, and I'm really too busy right now to help your organization."

You can redirect this conversation by saying, "I understand perfectly and appreciate your honesty. As long as I have you on the phone, let me ask you this: Who do you know who fits the profile that we should be talking to?" Often, this individual gladly suggests other prospects.

This simple turn of conversation changed a call that seemed to be going nowhere into a productive contact. Not only have you put your nonprofit's name and mission in front of a prominent individual, you've also learned the names of more potential sources. And you have a third-party referral to use when introducing yourself to these individuals.

■ **Abandoning the call.** If the prospect doesn't show any interest or enthusiasm toward you or the projects your nonprofit is working on, it's probably best to end the conversation.

Some people won't be interested, no matter how much telling and selling you do. If that is the case, don't pursue them. Pushing the issue will leave a bad taste in their mouths, which may prevent them from helping you on any future projects.

Move on after a negative contact

Sooner or later, all development team members will experience a "bad" contact. When this happens, do these two things:

First, learn something from the contact. Even though a phone call turns sour, there's always something useful to be gleaned from it. For example, you might decide to change a few words in the introduction or realize that a different transition from introduction to project description would be more inviting.

Second, move on to the next person on the list. The adage about getting right back on the horse that threw you off couldn't be more true than when it's applied to making telephone contacts.

Dwelling on the negatives of a call won't do any good—and it certainly won't help the development team find prospects worthy of pursuing. To do that, you must be constantly on the phone, contacting new people and telling them about your organization.

Action: When a contact goes bad, learn something from it, chalk it up to experience and then move on to the next challenge. There's no time to waste on things you can't change.

Use other recruitment tools to follow up telephone contacts

Following a positive recruiting contact with a thank-you note is good business sense. With the strategic recruiting process, however, you can take this gesture one step further.

Along with the thank-you note, enclose copies of your nonprofit's marketing piece/brochure and the position profile that you're recruiting for. Then if the prospect hasn't already agreed to a sit-down meeting, add a short message that says you'll call at a certain date and time to talk about the information. If the prospect has scheduled a meeting, simply write that you're looking forward to it and thought this information would help him or her prepare.

Sending this information gives prospects valuable insight about your nonprofit. The marketing piece/brochure tells them what the organization does and describes program goals. The position profile spells out in detail what would be expected from the individual if he or she becomes a board member. The end result is that candidates are in a better position to discuss the opportunity and make an informed decision about participating.

Dropping these items in the mail also distinguishes your nonprofit from others in the marketplace. Most organizations don't have these tools and are less likely to quickly pass along some well-organized background information and a specific outline of their needs. Because you can follow up with this additional information, your nonprofit will appear more organized, more professional and more enticing—especially to high-profile prospects.

Practice makes interviews perfect

Obviously, you wouldn't think of giving a speech or making an important presentation without practicing first. The same applies to the professional recruiting process!

Meet with other development team members to run through the presentation before meeting with prospective candidates. This way, you can decide who's going to say what, rehearse opening remarks, and time how long it takes to present your message.

As a result, board development team members can go into a meeting confident and relaxed. The "movie" of what's going to happen has already played in their minds. Since they know what is going to happen, they can concentrate less on what they plan to say and more on gathering information from the prospect.

❏ CONDUCT FACE-TO-FACE MEETINGS

Phase Two of the recruiting contact is a personal meeting between two or three board development team members and the prospective board member.

This meeting must be tightly structured, so prospects leave with a strong sense of your organization's goals, the recruiting process and what, exactly, you want from them. Specifically, you should…

■ **Hit the highlights of your nonprofit's story.** If you talked about the organization's goals during your initial phone conversation with the prospect—and followed up by sending him or her a copy of the position profile and the nonprofit's marketing piece/brochure—the prospect will already have a pretty firm grasp of who you are and what you're trying to accomplish.

To save meeting time, present only the highlights of the organization's story—with emphasis on how the prospect can help the nonprofit. Let's say the board's goal is to increase community awareness of the organization. If the prospect you're recruiting is part of the media, explain how you'd like to use his or her expertise and connections to improve public relations and build a more productive relationship with area media.

If the prospect has specific questions about the organization or its plans, answer them. However, try to limit the discussion of background to five to 10 minutes.

■ **Be clear about your expectations.** Don't beat around the bush about what you want from prospects.

Tell them up front that you want to walk away with two or three of their best referrals for the board position, or that you'd like them to personally consider the position. To high-profile individuals who are frequently asked to donate their time and money, forthrightness is impressive—and important.

■ **Explain the nonprofit's plans.** After telling prospects what you want from them, show them why you need their help.

This information will come from the organization's marketing piece/brochure. (Remember to concentrate on telling the features and selling the benefits.) Specifically, you should talk about the programs that prospects would be improving.

For example, explain how their expertise will enable the nonprofit to expand programs and serve more people. (This is the feature.) Then talk about how this service will help the community and improve the individual lives of those who participate in nonprofit programs. (This is the benefit.)

This helps create the emotional hook that makes it difficult for prospects to say "no." It also shows them that you have specific plans to use their expertise. Board service for them will be about actually doing something—not just attending meetings and listening to committee reports.

■ **Talk about the recruiting process.** Before closing, review the next steps in the recruiting process. An overview helps prospects understand what will be happening with this opportunity in coming months, and it reassures them that decisions don't have to be made immediately.

For example, explain to prospects that the next step is to familiarize them with the organization's programs and the people it serves. To do that, you'd like to invite them to attend a nonprofit event or committee work session. This will give both you and the prospect a chance to get to know each other better.

■ **Keep the meeting brief.** Most prospects are willing to set aside 45 minutes to an hour to meet with you. So you have to be organized and ready to start on time. Then conduct the meeting and leave on time.

Most board member prospects value their time. If you do the same—by beginning and ending on time—they will be far more impressed than if you arrive late, disorganized or run 15 minutes past your allotted time.

Let prospects share their feelings about the opportunity

At some point during your meeting with the prospect, you'll need to be quiet and listen to what the individual being recruited has to say. This is referred to as the "Golden Moment of Silence."

This moment usually evolves naturally. You'll either come to the end of your presentation and ask how the individual feels about what's just been said, or the prospect will ask questions or offer opinions as the conversation progresses.

At the conclusion of your presentation, ask a few simple questions about whether the prospect would be interested in helping the organization and, if so, what he or she would like to gain from the experience. Depending on the amount of time left for your appointment, you may also ask about the prospect's other board service experiences. What were they? What did he or she like and dislike?

Some of your questions will be generic, getting-to-know-you type questions. Others, however, should be based on the position profile. For example, dig into the prospect's experience and find out what, exactly, this individual has done in his or her career.

If prospects are interested in the opportunity—and you're interested in them—tell them that you'd like to continue getting to know each other at a nonprofit event or committee meeting. Then offer prospects another copy of the position profile and the organization's marketing piece/brochure and tell them that you'll soon be in touch to schedule another meeting.

Editor's Note: More about specific interviewing techniques is in Chapter 8.

When personal interviews go badly

Occasionally, you may find that a prospect is eager to help, but doesn't really have the background you're looking for.

These situations must be handled delicately, so you don't lose the individual's future support. Obviously, you don't want to say, "You're not qualified." This leaves a bad taste in the prospect's mouth and makes any kind of relationship with the prospect's organization or with him or her—whether it's as a donor, volunteer or future board member—impossible.

Here are some tactics that you can use to handle prospects who don't fit your criteria...

Tactic #1) State at the beginning of the interview that you're talking with several candidates. Prefacing your remarks with this statement leaves an escape door open in the event that a prospect isn't right for the board.

You've made it clear that others are being considered, and there are no implied commitments or guarantees. This initial meeting was solely for each of the parties to get to know one another, and to explore interests and specific qualifications.

Tactic #2) Leave them with copies of the position profile and nonprofit marketing piece. Most people are intuitive enough to know when they don't fit specifications. As you discuss the board position's requirements, emphasize what you're looking for. Then leave behind a copy of the position profile and marketing piece/brochure.

As a parting gesture, tell the person that you're in the process of identifying candidates and restate that you'll be talking with other prospects. Also let the individual know that this meeting was just a preliminary step in the recruitment process and that there are several others which follow. Finally, tell the prospect that you'll get back to him or her to talk about his or her level of interest.

Tactic #3) Invite them to serve on a committee rather than the full board. This is especially useful when the prospect has some of the experience you're looking for, but not as much as the ideal candidate.

For example, if you're looking for someone with marketing skills, you might tell the candidate during the meeting that you're really interested in someone with a few more years experience. You can add that you'd like to invite him or her to be part of the nonprofit's marketing committee.

This is a way of using the person's skills and involving him or her in the nonprofit without inviting him or her to serve on the board. It also gives the prospect a means to develop a relationship with the organization and learn how it operates. The prospect may ultimately become a donor or, a few years later after he or she has more marketing experience, assume a position on the full board.

Tactic #4) Invite them to attend other organization functions. If prospects are completely wrong for the position, you may want to begin steering them into other roles—such as volunteer or donor. Inviting them to attend a program or event would be a good way to ease them toward those alternatives.

❏ MAINTAIN RECORDS OF ALL CONTACTS

The board development team must keep records of prospect contacts and track overall activity. This is the only way to ensure that the team will do its job on a consistent basis.

Board development teams that aren't held to some kind of reporting schedule can easily slip back into the nominating committee way of doing things. Contacts will be put off until the last minute, and new members will join the board without being adequately evaluated.

Regular reports, however, force team members to show that they're actively collecting information. The pressure to report something keeps team members moving toward the recruitment goal.

Record information on Candidate Information Form

Every time you talk with a board member prospect, have a pen ready to take notes about his or her areas of expertise, experience, interest in board service and familiarity with your organization.

It's easiest to do this on a Board Candidate Information form. A copy of the information form is on Page 119. This form organizes information in a resume-style format, so it's easy for development team members to familiarize themselves with candidates and decide if they're right for the nonprofit.

Development team reports

Development team reports serve two purposes:

■ **Reporting to the team captain.** Before you begin the initial calling process, establish contact expectations and make a schedule for reporting results back to the development team. An ideal scenario would be for each team to make a minimum of two contacts per week and deliver copies of the relevant paperwork to the board development team captain every other week.

■ **Reporting to the full board.** The board development team captain will use members' reports to prepare the overall team report for the full board. This includes the number of contacts, the number of interviews and how many potential board members have been uncovered through these two steps.

Continuous contacts give development team a choice

Contacting prospective board members needs to be an ongoing process—not something that's done once a year, just before new members are installed.

This is vital to making the recruiting process work. If contacts aren't continuous, your organization won't be in a position of choice when it's time to add new members to the board.

The goal of strategic recruitment is to get the best possible board members—so the board can reach goals laid out in the nonprofit's strategic, operational and fund development plans. To match prospects' skills with your goals, evaluate all candidates, and then choose those who are most qualified.

Continuously contacting new prospects puts you in that position of choice because you always have several candidates moving through the evaluation process. And the contacts you make today or this week will replace the prospects who drop out of the process a month from now. You never end up in a situation where you have to take recruits you don't want because the best ones decided they weren't interested. ■

STOP! Procedure checkpoint

Before moving on to Step 8 of the strategic recruiting process, Evaluate and Select New Board Members, have you...

❑ Divided Board Recruiting Contact Sheets equally among development team members?

❑ Practiced making telephone contacts? (Pay attention to time, sales-like talk and third-party referrals.)

❑ Arranged personal meetings with interested prospects?

❑ Obtained referrals from prospects not interested in board service?

❑ Leveraged contacts to gain referrals to specific candidates?

❑ Left memories of failed contacts clearly in the past?

❑ Sent introductory letters to high-profile prospects?

❑ Followed through on what you stated in those letters?

❑ Sent the position profile and scripted story to interested contacts after talking with them on the telephone?

❑ Practiced making your presentation for personal meetings?

❑ Structured your presentation to be clear, informative and to the point?

❑ Met in groups with interested prospects?

❑ Answered prospects' questions about serving on your board?

❑ Made it clear that you're interviewing a number of different prospects?

❑ Recorded what was said during all contacts on the appropriate forms?

❑ Reported your individual group's contact results to the development team captain?

❑ Reported the development team's results to the full board?

❑ Continued contacting board prospects beyond the "initial need"?

BOARD RECRUITING CONTACTS

Name: _____   Comments: _____

Org: _____   _____

Pos: _____   _____

Date: _____   _____

Phone: (_____) _____   _____

Action: ❑ Recall   ❑ WCB   ❑ Intvw | Pass to: _____

Name: _____   Comments: _____

Org: _____   _____

Pos: _____   _____

Date: _____   _____

Phone: (_____) _____   _____

Action: ❑ Recall   ❑ WCB   ❑ Intvw | Pass to: _____

Name: _____   Comments: _____

Org: _____   _____

Pos: _____   _____

Date: _____   _____

Phone: (_____) _____   _____

Action: ❑ Recall   ❑ WCB   ❑ Intvw | Pass to: _____

Name: _____   Comments: _____

Org: _____   _____

Pos: _____   _____

Date: _____   _____

Phone: (_____) _____   _____

Action: ❑ Recall   ❑ WCB   ❑ Intvw | Pass to: _____

BOARD CANDIDATE INFORMATION

Name: _____ Date: _____

Address: _____

_____

Work phone: (_____) _____ Caller: _____

Home phone: (_____) _____

Organization: _____ Title: _____

Location: _____

Area of expertise:

Familiarity with our organization:

Interest in the board:

Referrals: _____ Next step: _____

_____

_____

Pass to:

❑ Nominating   ❑ Fund development   ❑ Marketing

❑ Other: _____

Résumé attached: ❑ Yes   ❑ No

CHAPTER 8

Evaluate and Select New Board Members

The evaluation process **125**
How to create contact and exposure 125
Questions reveal candidate qualities 126
Structured interviews provide results.. 126
Ask candidates to provide résumés 127
Present board member candidates with involvement options 127
Committees, short-term tasks get candidates involved 128
CASE STUDY: Value of strategic recruiting and flexibility 129
Long-term benefits of short-term project teams 129
When candidates want to immediately join the full board.................. 130
Select and recommend new members **131**
Candidate selection criteria 131
Recommend candidates to the board 131
First-time presentation expectations 132
Recommendations should be oral... 132
Board member installation basics 133
Evaluating the recruitment process 133
STOP! Procedure checkpoint 134
    Interview Question Exercise.. 135
    Recruitment Process Evaluation Form... 137

CHAPTER

Evaluate and Select New Board Members

Many development team members assume that a positive meeting with a board prospect means they should immediately extend an invitation to join the board. ■ Beware of first impressions! ■ Before asking anyone to join your board, put him or her through a thorough evaluation process. This helps you get to know the prospect and helps the prospect get to know you. And it will either confirm or negate the first impression that each of you formed during initial meetings. ■ For example, a candidate may be excited by the recruitment contact and impressed with development team members. After seeing the organization and the challenges facing it, though, this same prospect may decide that board service isn't what he or she wants. Conversely, other candidates may be skeptical at first, but grow interested when they see the outcome of the organization's programs and services. ■ The board development team is responsible for making sure a board member candidate is well-suited for the job. To do this, team members must continuously talk with prospects, show them around the facilities and ask them how they feel about being a board member. This chapter discusses the elements of an effective evaluation process and how to move prospects through it. ■

❏ THE EVALUATION PROCESS

"Contact" and "exposure" are key words in the recruitment and evaluation process. You need to maintain contact with qualified candidates and make sure they're exposed to the work your organization and board do.

When the board development team responds favorably to a candidate, the team members who initially met with him or her should start building a dialogue with that person. For example, team members should call the prospect to let him or her know what's happening with the organization and to talk more about how the prospect can help.

The development team should also try to get this individual into the nonprofit's facility as much as possible, so the prospect begins to appreciate the role your organization plays in the community. These visits give team members a chance to show the prospect the nonprofit's programs in action and the people they serve. Facility tours are also excellent opportunities to show a prospect how his or her expertise could correct a problem or improve service.

How to create contact and exposure

Here are three specific suggestions for drawing board prospects further into the evaluation process:

■ **Send them a letter of thanks.** Like initial telephone contacts with board member prospects, personal meetings should be followed up with a thank-you note. It's a sign of appreciation, and it shows the prospect that your nonprofit is interested in him or her.

A letter of thanks is also a perfect way to communicate your feelings about the meeting and suggest another get-together. This could be over lunch, dinner or during the workday. Or you can invite prospects to visit the nonprofit facility and see firsthand the services your organization provides.

■ **Invite them to nonprofit events.** If possible, accompany board prospects to a nonprofit event and introduce them as special guests of the board.

That could mean seating prospects at the board development team's table during a fund raising dinner, or accompanying prospects to some event, like a performance by the children your nonprofit serves.

■ **Invite them to committee work sessions.** Some nonprofits invite prospective board members to regular board meetings. While this is a good way to familiarize prospects with other board members and current board issues, it's not as productive as asking prospects to attend a board committee work session.

At a committee work session, the prospect sees exactly what he or she would be working on—and the people he or she would be working with. For example, take prospects being recruited for their fund raising expertise to a fund development committee meeting.

Prospects can see how the committee works, what it's trying to accomplish and how their background could be applied. This is far more exciting and informative for candidates than sitting through a board meeting.

Questions reveal candidate qualities

Whenever you spend time with a board member prospect, turn the opportunity into a working interview where you find out as much as possible about that person.

For example, ask prospects what kind of projects they're most interested in. That will help you determine if the prospect is someone who could meet the expectations specified in the position profile.

Be sure to ask open-ended questions. These are questions that can't be answered with a simple "yes" or "no." They're designed to give you information about the prospect by encouraging him or her to talk about personal interests and achievements. An excellent way to interview a candidate is to ask two or three open-ended questions and then listen to the answers. You'll quickly see whether this person would fit in with your board and what qualities he or she would bring to it.

Here are a few open-ended questions:

■ What do you do in your spare time?

■ What makes the organization worthy of a commitment of your time and money?

■ Why are you interested in the ballet, disadvantaged, disabled, etc.?

The interview question exercise on Pages 135-136 can help the board development team write questions that elicit important information from candidates.

Structured interviews provide results

All interview questions should be open-ended and asked in a way that allows you to compare candidates. This is called structured interviewing.

A well-structured interview is built around two elements: 1) goal-oriented questions; and 2) consistent interviewing techniques.

Goal-oriented questions are those designed to get the information you need. They can be "yes" or "no" questions, or they can be open-ended questions.

To build a set of goal-oriented questions, go back to the position profile for which you're recruiting. Review the experience and commitment level that you're looking for in a board member. Then write questions whose answers will reveal those qualities.

For example, some questions should be devoted to discovering if prospects have the professional background and skills you've identified. Others should focus on whether candidates will meet expectations, and some questions should zero in on the individual's energy level and integrity.

Ideally, you should prepare a list of 10 to 15 open-ended, goal-oriented questions.

The second element of a structured interview is interview technique. Basically, this means that you ask all candidates the same questions.

If candidates are asked different questions, comparing candidates and deciding who is best qualified becomes extremely difficult. For example, the board development team is trying to decide between two equally qualified candidates. Members decide that the tie-breaking issue should be the degree of commitment each candidate is willing to give.

One candidate is willing to serve at least one term, but won't guarantee attendance at all meetings. The other candidate, however, never indicated her commitment level because she was never asked.

This leaves the board development team

in the uncomfortable position of having to decide between a candidate who won't be at every meeting and a candidate whose commitment to attendance they have no idea about.

Either way, the development team will be taking an unnecessary chance. If members had asked the same questions of both candidates, they would have an objective way to make their choice.

Editor's Note: To be sure that everyone on the board development team is getting the same information from prospective board members, plan your interview questions the same way you write a position profile—as a group.

Ask candidates to provide résumés

It's also a good idea during the interviewing process to ask prospects for a copy of their résumé. This will give you additional insight into them and their skills.

Most prospects, especially high-profile ones, have no hesitation about providing you with a regular, employment-type résumé or other written biographical information. Your request for this information should come during the first or second contact.

When reviewing prospect résumés, look for the types of activities that indicate knowledge in a specific area. Also look for action-oriented activities that give clues about whether the individual has a track record of getting things done.

For example, positive indicators on a community relations professional's résumé might include conducting a campaign that increased customers' awareness by a certain factor, or showing a history of helping grow a company.

These action-oriented examples demonstrate that the prospect has proven skills—as well as enough intensity and drive to follow through with projects.

Present board member candidates with involvement options

The people you recruit are going to have good credentials. Not everyone, though, will turn out to be board member material.

Some candidates won't have the exact experience or expertise you're looking for, and others may lack connections in the community. A few just won't be interested. The evaluation process is about separating these prospects from more-qualified candidates.

Less-qualified candidates, however, shouldn't be "discarded." In fact, the exact opposite should occur.

Even though these individuals may not have the caliber of skills and resources that you need in a board member, their skills and resources can still benefit your organization. You can take advantage of this by offering less-qualified candidates other opportunities to help, such as:

■ **Having his or her name put on a list for future consideration.** This is an excellent way to handle the candidate whose skills are adequate, but who isn't the top talent you want on your board.

For example, you may be looking for a fund raising specialist. Several candidates are up-and-coming development directors with good fund raising track records, but they don't have connections to the community's major donors.

This is the type of candidates you'll probably pass over for now. But because these individuals show promise, you should stay in touch with them—with a promise to consider them for the board when they gain more experience.

The challenge here is to maintain your relationship with candidates while they grow in their profession. The best way to do this is to make candidates members of a nonprofit committee. The ideal committee in this case would be the organization's fund raising committee.

This strategy allows you to reap the benefits of the individuals' skills and begin building a "history" together. Later, when a board member position is open, these prospects will be primed and ready.

■ **Helping with short-term projects.** Some prospects—especially high-profile, highly accomplished ones—will express interest in your organization, but simply won't have the time or desire to commit to a full term on the board.

Don't consider this a rejection. Instead, offer them a short-term position—three to six months—on a current project committee.

If, for instance, your marketing committee is working on a new, long-term marketing plan, you could place one of these candidates on that team. You'll get the benefit of his or her experience, energy, skills and contacts, and the candidate will be able to make a valuable contribution without committing to a full board term.

This strategy has another benefit. As board member prospects participate in these projects, they form a relationship with your organization. And you're building a reservoir of names you can go back to and recruit from in the future.

■ **Becoming a donor.** This option is particularly useful when prospects aren't interested in board service or serving on a committee—but are impressed with the organization and its programs.

This is a win-win situation. The candidate gets emotional satisfaction from helping the people you serve, without the obligation of attending meetings or spending hours on a project. The nonprofit picks up financial support and adds a name to its donor list.

Committees, short-term tasks get candidates involved

If prospects meet the criteria established in the position profile and are interested in helping your board—and the board development team agrees that they would be valuable additions—the next step may be to get them involved in a project.

The best way to do this is to put candidates on committees that are working on short-term projects. Ideally, this should be the same committees that respective candidates would be involved with as board members.

You'll experience these benefits:

Benefit #1) It's an opportunity to see how prospects work. Until now, you only know board member candidates by what they've told you. You still have no idea what kinds of workers they are or how their work styles will fit in with other board members.

By having candidates work on a project, you'll find out how their personalities and work styles mesh with other committee members. In addition, these candidates will

---

CASE STUDY:
Value of strategic recruiting and flexibility

To illustrate the value of a flexible recruiting strategy, here's a story about a board candidate I know personally...

I had introduced him to two board development teams. One of the teams represented a young, developing organization. The other was part of a more mature nonprofit board.

Both teams approached this individual using the strategic recruiting process. After learning about both organizations, the candidate decided he wanted to join the older, more high-profile board.

Even though he turned down one board, both boards got what they were after here.

This individual was so impressed by the younger board's organization and programs that he agreed to donate his skills to it for six months. As a result, the nonprofit was able to capitalize on his marketing know-how and develop a new marketing plan.

These types of compromises aren't possible using the old method of recruiting, where joining the board is a candidate's only option. If the younger nonprofit had expected this individual to commit to long-term board service, as many nominating committees would have, it would have lost out altogether on benefiting from his expertise.

---

have an opportunity to meet board members other than those on the development team. This puts all board members in a much better position to either approve or reject proposed candidates. They can base their decisions on what they've observed about the candidate—not just on what they've read.

Benefit #2) It lets candidates put their skills to immediate use. Many candidates will be excited about the prospect of joining your board. Depending on when they were recruited, though, they may have to wait before they can be recommended as full board members.

Candidates' enthusiasm can easily fade during this waiting period. Involving them with committee work, however, keeps them interested and informed about what's happening with the organization. It's also an excellent way for the committee to benefit immediately from candidates' skills—rather than waiting until after they're installed as new members.

Long-term benefits of short-term project teams

As you recruit board prospects and volunteers, and place them on short-term project committees, you'll begin to notice a significant benefit of the professional recruiting process. Over time, finding qualified candidates for the full board—and getting them involved—becomes easier.

Some of this change is because development team members become more efficient with the process. Most of it, however, is the direct result of using both board prospects and volunteers as short-term committee members.

Because your organization will always have more total short-term committee members than full governance board members, adding new committee members means you're constantly building a surplus of board-caliber talent to recruit from. When it's time to bring new members onto the board, you can go to this talent pool—rather than starting the recruiting process all over again from scratch.

Short-term project committees also make it easier to get highly qualified board prospects to participate in your organization.

Some prospects won't be interested or able to serve full board terms because of busy schedules. You can still recruit these prospects—you just have to change your goal from recruiting this individual as a board member to a goal of recruiting this individual as a short-term committee volunteer.

This appeals to high-profile candidates who can't commit to a long-term board position. They can make a contribution to your organization, but won't be burdened by a meeting schedule and other board activities.

This strategy means that your nonprofit will reap the benefits of these volunteers' expertise—and it puts your development team in the most advantageous position possible to recruit these prospects again.

Each time a prospect makes a contribution to your organization—even if it's only a two-month term on a committee—it makes him or her feel good. And it helps the individual understand and appreciate the nonprofit's mission. This emotional hook may help lure the individual back for a longer term on the full board later on.

Eventually, this will lead to a change in your development team's overall recruiting strategy. Instead of going into the community to find recruits who are able to immediately join the board, the strategy will be to recruit candidates who can help with current short-term projects—but who have the potential later on to move into full board positions.

When candidates want to immediately join the full board

Most nonprofits have an ongoing need for qualified, results-oriented board members. Remember, the primary objective of the strategic board recruitment process is to identify, interest, evaluate and select individuals who will help the organization achieve stated objectives.

When the ideal candidate for a key open board position indicates interest in immediately joining the board, find a way to accommodate him or her. The board development team's charter is to "institutionalize" a professional recruitment process that continually identifies exceptional candidates for key volunteer and board positions. One way for nonprofits to distinguish themselves from others in the marketplace is to "hire" and effectively use the best professional and volunteer talent available.

❑ SELECT AND RECOMMEND NEW MEMBERS

The entire evaluation process should last several weeks, perhaps even months. At the end of this time, the board development team will decide who among the candidates should be invited to join the full governance board.

Candidate selection criteria

Several factors go into the decision about who deserves an invitation to become a full board member, including candidates' initiative, enthusiasm, commitment and overall chemistry with other board members. However, this decision should also be based on these three objective criteria:

■ **The position profile.** Profiles help you define what you're looking for, so it's easier to identify prospects at the beginning of the recruitment process. Now the position profiles will help you again—this time to identify the most-qualified candidate.

Profiles act as a sort checklist to see if candidates meet specified criteria. For example, does information gathered from the candidate indicate that he or she has the background and experience you're looking for? What about skills and expertise? Has he or she shown the willingness to meet your expectations?

■ **Work styles.** While candidates worked on their committees, how did they fit in with other board members? Were they organized and punctual? Did they meet deadlines and solve problems well? Overall, were they easy or difficult to work with? More importantly, are they someone the board would be happy to work with again?

■ **Goals.** Do candidates' goals match your organization's? If you're looking for someone to eventually be chairperson of your marketing committee, are these individuals willing to serve in leadership positions? Some candidates may prefer to serve only for a short time or help with a single project—instead of a full board term.

After deciding which candidates would make strong board members, the development team should formally invite them to join. If candidates accept your offer, tell them that you will be presenting their credentials to the full board. Candidates will be installed soon after the board approves the development team's recommendation.

Recommend candidates to the board

Although the board development team has done most of the recruiting work to this point, it lacks authority to actually bring new members onto the board. The power of approval still belongs to the full board.

That means the board development team must formally present its candidates to the full board. In this presentation, the team should walk board members through the whole recruitment process and then discuss why each nominee was selected.

To begin, the board development team should explain the goals and needs of the organization as they were determined during the assessment process. That should be followed by a brief recap of the position profile and then a short summary of each candidate's specific qualifications and why he or she is a good match for the job.

All board members should also receive a copy of the position profiles being voted on, all candidates' resumes and the Board Candidate Information forms that were kept for each prospect to help them reach a decision.

When presenting board candidates, the development team can take three different approaches to help the board make a decision. It can:

■ Present only the recommended candidates;

■ Present all candidates and let the full board choose; or

■ Present the entire group, but recommend some candidates.

The best strategy is to present only the top candidates. This is true for two reasons:

First, the board development team knows the candidates better than the full board. Therefore, development team members are in position to know who will benefit the board.

Second, presenting only recommended candidates simplifies the decision-making process. Rather than having to sift through a stack of paper and decide on their own, the remaining board members can rely on the judgment of the board development team.

First-time presentation expectations

The first few times your development team presents candidates to the full board, you should expect a lot of discussion.

Even though the process may seem fairly routine to team members at this point, it's still very new to the rest of the board. Members will have a lot of questions about the candidates and about the process—they'll want to test it, so to speak.

The best way to deal with this is to prepare thoroughly. Have all notes made about the candidates available, and be familiar with their backgrounds. Then answer all board members' questions openly and honestly.

It's also good to divide the presentation among the board development team members. This allows everyone to give his or her input about the process and how the candidates have been identified and selected.

After the first two or three candidate presentations, the board will have had the opportunity to see the positive results of the strategic recruitment process. Board members should have more confidence in the system, and questions about candidates and their qualifications will be fewer.

Recommendations should be oral

When presenting board member candidates to the full board, one thing you should not do is put your recommendation in writing.

Instead, let board members base their decisions on candidates' résumés and Board Candidate Information forms. Members should be able and willing to have a full and complete discussion of the assets and liabilities of all candidates.

Doing this makes it easier to explain yourself in the unlikely event that a candidate asks why he or she wasn't chosen to serve on the board. You can tell the individual that all candidates were presented to the board in a similar manner, and the final approval decision was left up to board members.

Board member installation basics

Nominees who are approved must be formally installed, like all other members of the board.

Because strategic recruiting is a year-round activity, it's a good idea to install new board members twice a year. One installment can be held in January, as many installations traditionally are. A second should be held in the middle of the year, perhaps in June.

Holding two installation ceremonies will help prevent candidates who are invited early in the year to join the board from losing interest. This is especially true when the time lapse is more than two or three months. Someone chosen in March for the full board will still be enthusiastic about the job in June, but may have all but forgotten about it by December.

Even with a twice-yearly installation schedule, though, some candidates will still have to wait before taking their board seats. To maintain their enthusiasm, involve them immediately on the committees they'll be assisting. Ask them to attend board meetings so they'll be up-to-speed on the issues as soon as they're installed.

Editor's Note: New member installation is a topic usually described in a board's bylaws. Before adopting the biannual installation process, be sure to adjust your bylaws to accommodate these changes.

Evaluating the recruitment process

Like all other processes and events conducted by your board, the recruitment process should be evaluated. This is the best way to improve the process and make it even more effective in the future.

The best time to do your initial evaluation is after one full cycle (beginning with defining a position and ending with installment). And again, the board development team is responsible for completing this task.

To evaluate the process, answer these three questions:

■ What's working and should remain the same?

■ What's not working and how can it be improved?

■ Who's going to make the necessary improvements and when will this be accomplished?

Use the same procedure to evaluate the recruitment process that you used to evaluate the board. Development team members should complete an evaluation individually and then discuss their feelings as a group.

Editor's Note: An evaluation form is on Page 137.

STOP! Procedure checkpoint

Before moving on to further activity using the strategic recruiting process, have you...

❑ Talked with the board development team about how to move prospects through the evaluation process?

❑ Thanked prospects who met personally with you?

❑ Invited prospects to visit the organization's facility?

❑ Invited prospects to attend board committee work sessions?

❑ Prepared a list of open-ended interview questions based on the position profile?

❑ Coordinated your interview questions with other development team members?

❑ Asked board member candidates to provide résumés?

❑ Told lesser-qualified candidates of their involvement alternatives?

❑ Placed qualified candidates on short-term committees or project teams?

❑ Evaluated how candidates worked in these committee and team situations?

❑ Organized selection criteria to choose new board members?

❑ Decided how the team will present candidates to the board and prepared an appropriate presentation?

❑ Evaluated the recruitment process?

INTERVIEW QUESTION EXERCISE

Use this sheet to brainstorm possible interview questions that will alert the board development team to specific qualities and experience it is seeking in a board member candidate. Develop open-ended questions beginning with the following words...

What...

Where...

When...

Why...

How...

RECRUITMENT PROCESS EVALUATION FORM

After one full cycle of board member recruitment using the Strategic Board Recruitment Model, please answer the following questions:

1. What about the process is working and should remain the same?

2. What about the process is <u>not</u> working, and how can it be improved?

Element not working	Improvement ideas

3. Who's going to make the necessary improvements, and when will this be accomplished?

Task(s)	Person responsible	Due date
_____	_____	_____
_____	_____	_____
_____	_____	_____
_____	_____	_____
_____	_____	_____

❏ IN SUMMARY

Congratulations! You've just strategically identified, recruited and selected your first class of new board members. And you've laid the groundwork for a higher quality board in the future.

The new board members you've just installed know your organization's goals, and they know what their role will be in reaching them. But more importantly, they also know what your recruitment process is all about.

In the future, these newly recruited board members will expect other board prospects to go through the same rigorous selection and evaluation process. They will want to know that all prospects have the skills to meet the challenges facing the organization. That means two things for you—an ever-improving and effective board, and growing programs and services.

In other words, you've just taken the first steps toward institutionalizing your professional recruitment process.

❏ ABOUT THE AUTHORS

Robert W. Kile

Bob is Vice President and Partner at Rusher, Loscavio & LoPresto, a San Francisco and Palo Alto, California, based executive search firm. As managing partner of the nonprofit practice, Bob's interests and expertise include recruiting senior executives and building nonprofit boards.

He received his BBA from Western Michigan University and completed a two-year postgraduate program at the General Motors Institute. His 32 years of experience include key human resource management assignments with General Motors, Verbatim and Matson Navigation, as well as Founder/President of a San Francisco-based executive search and consulting firm.

As a keynote speaker and consultant, he has presented the Strategic Board Recruitment Model to thousands of conference participants, executives and board members including the 1994 NSFRE International Conference, the California Society of C.P.A.s, University of San Francisco Institute for Nonprofit Organization Management, YMCA, American Red Cross, Goodwill, Asian Pacific American Foundation, National Hispanic Scholarship Foundation, Oakland Ballet, Summit Medical Center Foundation and Leadership America. He volunteers his leadership skills to numerous local and national nonprofit boards.

J. Michael Loscavio

Mike is currently Vice President and Senior Partner at Rusher, Loscavio & LoPresto, and has been with the firm since its inception in 1977. He received a BA from San Diego State University and a Master's Degree in Management from the University of Nebraska. He is currently a faculty member and Director of the Golden Gate University Executive MBA program.

Mike has served as United States Representative and Foreign Liaison Officer to the United Nations Command in Tokyo, working with the Japanese Foreign Office and major Tokyo embassies. He spent four years as Strategic Planner and Project Manager for the National Scientific Advisory Group, consulting staff on domestic and foreign nuclear systems, and he was a consultant with a large executive search firm in Chicago.

Mike is an active member of San Francisco's Business Arts Council and the Business Volunteers for the Arts. He helps establish, expand and strengthen boards of directors for some of San Francisco's leading arts and nonprofit organizations. Mike has also been a featured speaker at the Commonwealth Club of San Francisco on employment issues in the 1990s. He has served on nonprofit boards in education and the arts.